JOURNEY OF AN IMMIGRANT

THE AMERICAN DREAM

SAISNATH BAIJOO

Order this book online at www.trafford.com
or email orders@trafford.com

Most Trafford titles are also available at major online book retailers.

© Copyright 2014 Saisnath Baijoo.

All rights reserved. No part of this publication may be reproduced, stored in a retrieval system, or transmitted, in any form or by any means, electronic, mechanical, photocopying, recording, or otherwise, without the written prior permission of the author.

Printed in the United States of America.

ISBN: 978-1-4907-3423-1 (sc)
ISBN: 978-1-4907-3424-8 (hc)
ISBN: 978-1-4907-3425-5 (e)

Library of Congress Control Number: 2014907547

Because of the dynamic nature of the Internet, any web addresses or links contained in this book may have changed since publication and may no longer be valid. The views expressed in this work are solely those of the author and do not necessarily reflect the views of the publisher, and the publisher hereby disclaims any responsibility for them.

Any people depicted in stock imagery provided by Thinkstock are models, and such images are being used for illustrative purposes only.
Certain stock imagery © Thinkstock.

Trafford rev. 05/07/2014

 www.trafford.com

North America & international
toll-free: 1 888 232 4444 (USA & Canada)
fax: 812 355 4082

Dedication

To my parents and family, who were my inspiration. They taught us that education is the key to liberation.

To every immigrant working towards the American dream.

To the workers of the healthcare sector, who work tirelessly every day to provide first-class professional service.

CONTENTS

Chapter One: Our Journey Begins: Reflections of My Beloved Trinidad 1
Chapter Two: Broken Promises, Concept of the Living Dead 17
Chapter Three: Good News: It Is Back to Miami 43
Chapter Four: My Pharmacy Training Begins 57
Chapter Five: Disaster Strikes Hard 70
Chapter Six: Education Is the Key to Your Salvation and Liberation 84
Chapter Seven: A New Adventure 93
Chapter Eight: Failure Strikes Hard from Within and Without 111
Chapter Nine: The Strategy for Success: Home Run 121
Chapter Ten: Deception and Divorce 130
Chapter Eleven: Strategy to Avoid Financial Disaster ... 147
Chapter Twelve: Journey to Roots 162
Chapter Thirteen: Adaptation to Changes 187
Chapter Fourteen: Love Blooms 203
Chapter Fifteen: Capturing the American Dream 230

Glossary 247

CHAPTER ONE

Our Journey Begins: Reflections of My Beloved Trinidad

He waved sadly as I bade my final farewell. Tears streamed down his wrinkled face. There were tears of joy that his son was migrating to live the American dream. There were tears of sadness and uncertainty.

He pondered whether he would live to see his son again. He hugged me tightly with his fragile yet robust body. He looked at me sternly, as tears poured from his eyes, and said, "Do not forget your roots and your culture. Do not be a living dead in America. Make a meaningful impact on the American society. Always help those that need help even in the smallest way."

I shook my head in acknowledgment of his wise advice. Then I reached down and touched my parents' feet as a mark of respect and reverence for their guidance and for sheltering me from all troubles throughout my life.

He continued very emotionally, "I may not see you again. America is now your adopted country. Do not look back. If you look back, you will fail in your endeavors. Capture the American dream. I know you are determined to conquer anything. You must love and respect everyone. Be humble, but be strong. Being humble does not make you weak. In fact, it sets your life to a different level in the sight of God."

My parents are my mentor and heroes. They are my rock of Gibraltar in my life. They molded my life with a solid foundation. It seems like a whole village had come to Piarco International Airport to say their last farewell. My five sisters, my four brothers, and their children were all at the airport.

The previous night, they had organized a farewell party for my family and I.

It was a very sad and emotional time at the airport. They were all sad but happy for my family and me. My name is Moonan. My parents' names are Baijoo and Kowsillia. This is my story. It is a journey into life.

This is the journey of an immigrant in search of the American dream. With tear-filled eyes, I turned to my parents and said, "I will make you proud. My heart and prayers will always be with you all. How can I forget the best parents in this world? You sacrificed your life to make me happy. You molded me to be strong. You are my life."

Then my son Jewan spoke to me, saying, "Your absence here will create a big vacuum in my life. I do not want to lose that loving and harmonious relationship that we have presently. You will always be my father who means the world to me. I will miss you."

He hugged me tightly as if it was our last farewell.

Our time to go through Immigration was quickly approaching, so I spoke to everyone before departing.

My voice quivered while I spoke, saying, "We have always been a close family. My life is not complete without every one of you. Therefore, we must not lose that bond. When we lose that close bond with each other, we lose the essence of living. I promise that I will call you all as often as possible."

Everyone wanted a farewell embrace.

I hugged my son tightly for the last time. Tears streamed down my face, and I said, "I will miss you. Please focus on your university studies. That is priority in your life. Do not forget the good times that we had together."

He nodded his head, acknowledging my request.

My two eldest daughters, Hema and Puja, were anxious to board the plane on their new adventure.

Hema shouted, "Let us go, Daddy, before the plane leaves us."

They are my two eldest daughters. They can light up any dull moment with their zest for life and their comical nature. My wife, Sandra, and our baby Mala was also coming. We waved our last farewell to all our families and well-wishers.

We boarded the plane amid heightened security.

There was an eerie silence and a certain nervous tension inside the plane. The repercussion was because of 9/11. Everyone was worried whether there will be other attacks. Just a month before, we had seen the senseless and vicious terrorist attack on my adopted country. My father always taught me that all forms of life are sacred. We cannot create life, so we should not destroy it. I sat on the plane and reflected: *What a wanton waste and disregard for life! Surely, these terrorists had families or children of their own.* The flight left Trinidad without any problems or delays.

My family had fallen asleep. I could tell by their familiar snoring sounds. They had enjoyed themselves throughout the previous night at a farewell party at my brother's home.

Suddenly, the plane was shaking vigorously. My heart skipped a beat. Then the pilot said, "Ladies and gentlemen, this is your pilot speaking. We are experiencing unusual turbulent weather. Please, under no condition should you leave your seats. Flight attendants, go to your seats at once."

The pilot had not finished speaking when suddenly; the plane plummeted in altitude as though it was out of control. Everyone was either screaming or praying. My family was still sounding asleep. They were unperturbed as the plane was tossed helplessly. The plane was tossed like a little ragged doll in the turbulent weather. The luggage bins were opening, and a few suitcases fell on unsuspecting passengers. This horrible ordeal continued for about an hour. All the passengers were traumatized every minute into this terror flight. One minute there were shouts of fear, and then there was a deadly silence. There were abrupt and periodic ascending and descending of the plane. After about three hours, the pilot announced that the rest of the flight would be smooth. Everyone was visibly shaken by this ordeal. My family slept throughout the whole ordeal. Then the pilot announced that we were landing in half an hour. Everyone was elated. I awoke my sleepy family from their very deep slumber.

It was time to get prepared for landing. We hurriedly departed from the plane and proceeded through Immigration. Notably absent was laughter or joy coming from the arriving passengers to the land of the free. When we reached the line, the Immigration officer looked at the documents and said, "Please follow the officer to the other room. We have to verify some information."

My family was terrified. Sandra, my wife, asked, "What is going on? Are you sure that all our relevant documents are in order?"

"Everything will be all right. God takes care of his people. Do not worry. Everything will be all right. Besides, I rechecked all our documents a few times" was my hesitant reply.

Somehow, those words did not provide comfort to anyone at that time.

We were hastily escorted into a waiting room that was full of distressed passengers.

It was a pitiful sight. There were many worried faces in that detention room. Some of the detained passengers were crying uncontrollably.

This made us think that something was definitely wrong with our Immigration documents. Why were we detained? We approached the officer sitting at the desk. I tried to ask the officer what the problem was with our documents. He was visibly upset and said, "I will call you when I am ready. Until then, have a seat. No unnecessary talking, and do not use a cell phone."

I was simply trying to tell him that we needed to change our baby Mala's diapers. We needed to use the restroom.

We saw people come after us, and their names were called, but there was no word from the dedicated officers about our concerns.

We were detained for seven hours without an explanation. After this time, the officer summoned us, waving our documents in his hand and saying, "You all may leave now."

There was no explanation or apology from anyone as to the reason for our detention. I told my family, "It is better to be sure and secure."

From Trinidad to Miami and Immigration, it normally takes about four-and-a-half hours.

This time, it took eleven-and-a-half hours. We left the airport, visibly upset. By now, the sun was peeping through the glorious morning skies. We boarded a taxi and headed for the Best Western hotel. Everyone was tired and upset. No one wanted to discuss the unmannerly welcome that we received to the United States of America.

At the Best Western hotel, my family booked into one room. We had to save money because we did not know when I would be employed. I dozed off on the couch.

My mind ran back to our beloved Trinidad. I was born in a small village in Trinidad called Caroni village. It was a beautiful and scenic area.

The Caroni River meanders gracefully on its borders. Lush green bamboo trees, poui trees, and variety of multicolored trees surround this scenic area. They add to the tranquil beauty of the area. My forefathers were conned into coming from India to Trinidad by their British colonial masters. They were brought to the West Indies as slaves or the glorified term "contract workers." When they reached the West Indies, their status changed to slaves. They were beaten and battered in the most inhumane way possible. They lived in tents called barracks. They lived in the most deplorable conditions.

My parents, like their parents, worked in the sugar plantations. They worked from dusk to dawn. As a child, my brothers and sisters assisted my parents in cutting and loading the canes onto carts. The cane was weighed and then transported to the sugar mills to make sugar or alcohol. Therefore, child labor was legal. The British slave masters cursed and abused the last drop of dignity from a humble but proud people.

My parents always dreamed about going back to Mother India. However, with their meager wages, that dream was impossible. Their family had migrated from the ancient land of Bihar, India.

The history of Bihar is as old as human civilization. This was the land where Lord Buddha attained enlightenment. One of the first universities for higher learning is located in Bihar.

The birthplace of Mother Sita is located in Punaura, Bihar. The author of the great epic *Ramayana-Valmiki* lived in Bihar.

With my parents, there was no time for a formal education. They just wanted to survive and maintain their children to a higher standard of living. My parents instilled in our mind, saying, "Do not stay in the cane fields. Do not be slaves like us. Get out from the sugarcane fields. There is no future here. Get an education and liberate yourself from the shackles of slavery. Look at your parents and rise above their status."

In the sugar estates, there was no break for meals. You ate while you were working. Despite all the hard labor, my parents still found time to raise ten children. My parents' concept was that their children were their wealth. It was comical that they nicknamed the British supervisor, Satan. The name, of course, refers to the devil in Christian doctrines.

This name, of course, was used when he was not in their presence. The British masters coerced the indentured slaves to abandon their culture, language, and religion.

They were hell-bent on converting all Indian slaves to Christianity. The idea was to totally transform the Indians to the British way of life. In return for conversion, they promised the Indians better jobs and schooling for the family. My parents believed that all religions were the same, so converting was like jumping from one fire to another.

My father proudly said, "I was born a Hindu, and I will die as one. Nothing that the British offers us will make me change my way of living."

My father had a good sense of humor. He said, "A newly converted Christian Indian from Hinduism invited his priest on Easter Friday for lunch. He served chicken to the priest. The priest was visibly upset. He told the new convert, 'Brother, at Easter time, it is customary that you serve fish, not chicken. You have to leave your old practices behind and move forward.' The new convert told the priest, 'Father, I am confused. You converted me from Hinduism to Christianity. Then surely you can convert the chicken to fish.'"

My father, even without a formal education, knew quotations from the Hindu Bible (the Bhagavad Gita). One such quotation was, "Whatever and whichever way men approach me (God), and even so do I accept them. Whatever pathways a believer may choose, finally lead to me. Again, in whatever form a devotee seeks to worship me with faith, I will make his faith steadfast in that form alone."

In my parents' tranquil world, God was simple. "It does not matter whether you call God by the name of Jesus or Allah or Ram. There is one God—only the names are different. All scriptures are inspiration of God. It is your personal devotion, faith, and love to God that is important. That is the key to the kingdom of heaven. God said, 'If anyone offers me with love and devotion a leaf, a flower, a fruit, or water, I will accept it.' Look at all the streams, rivers, and lakes. They eventually flow into one ocean. Faith in God is the same concept. When you say that you love God, then you help people in need. That is the essence of living."

My parents were unperturbed by the many forces and propaganda to convert them to Christianity. They were unwavering in their desire to perform puja or prayers that were handed down from their forefathers. My parents were poor, but they invited the neighbors to share in the little food that they prepared for their family.

The whole village was one big family. They shared in the joy and suffering of every neighbor. My father told me once,

"Look around at this prayer. There are Hindus, Muslims, and Christians. When you say that any one religion is the best, you blind yourself from the rest of the world. Do not grow up to be narrow-minded. Do not blind yourself from enjoying every culture. Look at the colors of the rainbow—that is a reflection of life. God sends that rainbow to remind us that the world is multicolored. No color in the rainbow is superior to the other one. Everyone here lives like a family, and that is what God wants in this life. He wants us to live with love and in harmony. That is the essence of salvation."

Growing up as a child in Caroni Village, all the neighbors cared and loved you like a big family.

They were never afraid to discipline you with a leather belt or a bamboo stick.

If your neighbor disciplined you and you complained to your parents, then you would get another beating. The whole village was one family unit. Everyone helped each other. When my mother helped a neighbor with their cooking, we had a free meal there.

My father's religion, Hinduism, taught him, "All men are equal. It does not matter what creed or race you were born into or your family. That is fate, and you have no choice in the matter. Wealth or money is Maya, or illusion. It does not guarantee happiness."

He continued, "If you want to conquer the world, embrace all philosophy and all scriptures."

My father was very strong physically. After working in the sugarcane fields, he still found time to fish with his children and plant a variety of crops.

Most of the crops he shared with the neighbors.

When the neighbors harvested their crops, they shared it with us. The bordering Caroni River was abundant with a variety of fishes, lobsters, and crabs. My brothers and sisters spent many pleasurable moments fishing. Every fishing expedition was a competition between family members. Everyone wanted to brag as to who will catch the biggest fish.

My mother was adamant that all her children receive a proper formal education. She knew their weaknesses and how to overcome poverty.

She said adamantly, "Your education is your salvation. Without a proper education, you would be like a dog in the streets. There would be no hope for your future. Take advantage of improving yourself. Reach for the skies. That is your limit. We have suffered without a formal education. Learn from our mistakes."

Thankfully, all her children listened to her advice, and they marched out of the cane fields.

Every one of my brothers and sisters received a formal education. There was no turning back to the sugarcane fields.

In 1962, Trinidad and Tobago achieved independence from their colonial masters. The country was free to travel its own destiny. Like most departing colonial powers, the British left the country on the brink of bankruptcy. My fellow countrymen were determined to make their newly acquired independence an example to the world. In Caroni village, the people were rejoicing in the streets. Their cruel supervisor, Satan, was going back to England.

As the national flag, with the colors of red, white, and black of Trinidad and Tobago, was hoisted, the citizens sang, "Where every creed and race find an equal place, and may God bless our nation."

The shackles of slavery was now a monument of the past.

CHAPTER TWO

Broken Promises, Concept of the Living Dead

I was anxious to contact Mr. Pat at Hurts Rx Pharmacy. He was the reason that I migrated to Florida in search of a new job and, henceforth, a new life. While in Trinidad, we had spoken on the telephone on a few occasions regarding my training as a pharmacist intern.

He had previously said, "No problem, just come over to Florida. We have many jobs for pharmacist interns now. When you are in Miami, just call me, and I will arrange an interview for you. Your work here is guaranteed with this company. Just call me as soon as possible."

With high expectations, I rushed down to the lobby of the hotel, armed with my Hurts Rx Pharmacy acceptance letter in hand. My plan was simple: inform Mr. Pat that I had arrived in Miami, and start working as early as possible.

He had given me his cell phone number on the acceptance letter. With high expectations, I hurriedly dialed his number.

He answered his cell phone, "Hi, this is Pat. Can I help you?"

"Good morning, Mr. Pat. This is Moonan from Trinidad. How are you, sir? I am here in Miami. You said that you would have a job for me as pharmacy intern when I reach here. Well, sir, my family has migrated to Florida. I am here just as we discussed on the phone."

Mr. Pat replied, "Moonan . . . I do not know anyone by that name. Anyway, presently, we, as a company, are not hiring pharmacy interns. Can you call me back in six months? Then we might have vacancies. I am very busy at this moment."

My desperation was overwhelming me. My heart started to palpitate with this traumatic news.

"Sir, please, please, understand my dilemma. I have no one to turn to for help except you. Without a job, I would have to return to Trinidad. Sir, I have a letter signed by you, and we spoke on the telephone on three occasions regarding my employment. Please, I am begging you to help me."

With that final word, Mr. Pat hung up the telephone; even after redialing, there was no answer. My hope of survival without gainful employment was impossible. Mr. Pat had given me so much hope in his letters and personal conversations that I did not investigate a second plan of action. I felt rejected as if there was no hope for tomorrow.

This pharmacy supervisor had no passion and love for helping me even though I had a confirmation letter for a work in his pharmacy. I felt like crying or screaming. My mother would say screaming will not help; actually, it makes it worse, and the problem is still there.

She said, "With prayer and faith, God is going to help you beyond your understanding. Always be kind and helpful even when people are not kind to you. One day, God may come in the form of a beggar or a sick person to test your goodness and kindness. Even when the clouds are hazy, look for a silver lining. Even when circumstances are vague and disappointing, look at the positive side and not the negative. Do not blame God for your weakness and failures."

Even with these comforting words, my mind could not comprehend how deceptive people can become after giving their word. Mr. Pat clearly stated in his letter that I would be employed when I arrive in Miami. Walking helps me to relax the mind, so I decided to take a stroll around the hotel. At the poolside of the hotel, there were people enjoying themselves. It was a joyous sight to see people relaxing and at ease with the world.

I wanted some consolation, but I was a stranger in this vast land, without a friend. Then I remembered that my teacher and mentor from Trinidad, Dr. Ravi, had given me the telephone number for his friend living in Florida.

Dr. Ravi had said to me, "Moonan, this phone number is of my friend Moe. He is like a brother from another mother to me. Whatever problems you encounter, call Moe. Call him, and just talk about any information that you need. He will help, and you can trust him with anything."

In desperation, I walked quickly back to the phone booth to call Mr. Moe. After my traumatic discussion with Mr. Pat, I wanted someone to listen to my dilemma and offer any advice. I called Moe and introduced myself as a friend of Mr. Ravi. I told him about the problems and my shattered dreams of not working at Hurts Rx Discount Pharmacy.

Moe said, "Any friend of Ravi is a friend of mine. Whatever I can do for you, I shall. Tell me. I am here for you, my brother. It is not a good situation. I know a lot of people who are promised jobs just like you."

Tears filled my eyes, and I said, "I do not know what to do at this moment. Without a job, my family will soon have no money to pay for anything. I am lost and need help desperately. We do not know anyone in Florida."

Moe's suggestion was simple. "Hey, my friend, you can bring your family to my home in Naples and stay here until you resolve your problems. I am going to work toward helping you get a job."

My half-hearted reply was, "But I have do not have transport to come there. I have no idea where Naples is located. How does my family reach Naples? We are presently staying at Best Western hotel in Kendall."

Moe was laughing heartily at my ignorance of my location.

He added, "Relax, it is only a two-hundred miles journey. If you want, I can come in the morning and bring you to my hotel. It is only about three hours' drive one way. Check out at eleven in the morning, and I will be there promptly."

For a brief moment, I was at a loss for words. Was this conversation real, or was the same thing going to happen as the case with Mr. Pat? What were my choices? There was no other contingency plan.

I was moved at his kindness, and I said to him, "Thank you for your help. My family needs your help and support. We have no one to help us here. We will be waiting for you in the hotel lobby."

On reaching my apartment, my family was informed of the bad news and my alternative plans.

The next morning, Moe was punctual. My family was finally meeting him. Dr. Ravi in Trinidad had spoken so highly of Moe during his stay in Florida. He had a broad smile that advertised his white glossy teeth. His hair was black with a touch of gray. He was a handsome middle-aged man. He was muscular and well-built as if he visited the gym on regular intervals.

He walked up to me with confidence and said, "Good morning, and my friend. How are you? This must your family. It is a long drive. Let us leave right now. We will get acquainted as we are on the road." All our suitcases were packed quickly into his Toyota four-runner, and our unplanned journey to Naples had begun. Our lives had been pushed into a new direction. Normally, my life is planned with organized fixed schedules. However, that day, I could not foresee where or what my next step in life would go or what would be the outcome. This kind of scenario was unfamiliar to me. Life is uncertain most of the times. We just have to trust God and hope the end serves our purpose. Presently, we were happy that we had new friend who was keen in helping us during this most desperate time. Moe was aptly dressed for the hot and humid Florida weather. His wear was casual. He wore brown short pants with a matching jersey and slippers. On the other hand, my outfit showed my ignorance of the Florida weather. My dress was a long-sleeved shirt and non-matching long pants. Of course, I wore thick socks and leather shoes. I had to adapt to dressing for the Florida weather. My body was sweating profusely, whereas Moe was as cool as a cucumber.

We proceeded with our long journey.

Moe said, "My children love to play this game when we have new friends at our home. You are going to tell us about yourself, or this will be a boring trip. I am from Trinidad in a place call Couva. My father worked in planting rice. We also had a cattle ranch. They worked for a big company. They were poor people but were very happy.

"They had a home built from wood, mud, and rice straw. That house was never hot. It was as cool as a cucumber or like an air-conditioned room.

"When my wife and I got married, we migrated to the United States. This is our home.

"America is our home. We love it here, and we will not exchange it for anywhere in the world. I am a Muslim, and my wife is a Hindu. We celebrate all cultures and festivals."

Moe spoke nonstop for about twenty minutes, and we listened attentively.

He laughed and joked about anything and everything. I wondered whether Moe had any problems. When we dwell on the negative aspects of life, it affects our mental and physical well-being.

Sai Baba said, "When the mind is sick, the body becomes sick."

My mind was dwelling on the negative. That was not good for my health.

Moe then said, "Ladies first. What about you, Sandra? Tell us about yourself."

My wife started, "I am from Moruga. My parents planted cocoa and coffee for their living.

"Moruga is one of the oldest towns in Trinidad. It is said to be the place where Christopher Columbus landed when he rediscovered Trinidad. Hema, one day you will tell the true story of a sperm whale. This beautiful giant from the sea was stranded in the shallow waters in Moruga. Hema actually touched the whale on the beach. Moruga is known for the hottest chili peppers in the world."

Everyone laughed when Sandra said that the hottest peppers came from Moruga.

Moe interrupted, saying, "I know you guys are worried, but relax. Everything will work out for the best. You have one life to live, so live it to the fullest. Problems make you stronger, so fight to be strong. Never give up."

Moe sounded like a philosopher.

My family welcomed this unplanned trip. I do not think they cared where they were going. A journey through uncertainty was not their worry. I told myself to get rid of my sulky mood and enjoy the company of my new friend. My children were certainly enjoying themselves. Then I thought that I should be happy too and enjoy our time together. If I am sad, then that will distress them. As parents, we must not burden our children with unnecessary problems that we encounter daily. Their time will come, so let them enjoy their childhood days. We must shield them from the pressures that we undergo daily.

With a deep breath, I decided to be positive and leave all my problems for another day.

My children were tossing many questions to Moe.

He was enjoying the chatter from my daughters.

Moe continued, "This is the Everglades. This is the home of the most exotic wildlife. There are many majestic birds that live in this sanctuary. Here, you will see the biggest alligator, crocodiles, and snakes in the world. There are videos online of larger snakes swallowing six-foot crocodiles. Everglades is home to a lot of manatees, fishes, and panthers."

Hema and Puja stopped their chatting and listened attentively. They were shocked at what they were hearing. There was total silence inside the vehicle. Moe continued, "In the Everglades, you have to be extremely vigilant. Anything can happen. There is so much exotic wildlife here, but it is a very dangerous place."

Hema and Puja were on the edge of their seats. They were frightened at what they were hearing.

Suddenly and without warning, a huge crocodile emerged from the murky waters. He was trying to cross the road but was in the direct path of an oncoming eighteen-wheeler truck. Moe realized that the driver of the eighteen-wheeler did not see the oncoming crocodile. In desperation, Moe blew his horn repeatedly but in vain. The creature was in the direct path of the truck, but the driver never responded on time. The truck ran over the head of the gigantic crocodile. The driver slammed on the brakes, causing his massive vehicle to swerve and block all traffic on both lanes. Moe had foreseen this danger and had pulled to the extreme shoulder of the road. The ripple effect of this action was that cars were crashing into each other. Moe jumped out of his vehicle and went to the assistance of the other drivers. Hema, Puja, and I followed close behind him.

The creature was grimacing in pain. There was a groaning sound as if a human being was in pain.

There were tears and blood streaming down his crushed eyes. It was a gruesome sight. The creature was bleeding profusely. It was like a murder scene in an R-rated movie. Everyone who witnessed this horrific incident left with tears in their eyes. Traffic was backed up for a mile. The Fire Department had arrived. They were desperately trying to dislodge the mangled crocodile from the truck. Moe motioned us to leave immediately as the traffic was building up to a massive pileup.

There was an eerie silence inside the vehicle as we departed. Everyone was visibly shaken by the tragic incident.

Moe, sensing the sadness, said, "Hema, it is your turn. Tell me about yourself."

A smile returned to Hema's face. She loves to talk about herself and her ambitions. "I went to the same high school as my dad. I did very well in school. I love sports, and I love to fish with my father. I remember as it was yesterday fishing in the Caroni Swamp with my dad. We caught many fishes together. That was fantastic."

Puja interrupted, saying, "Yes, and there were alligators, but Dad took us fishing anyway. We had fun because my father's friend took all his children fishing too. We enjoyed these trips immensely. The Caroni Swamp, like the Everglades, is one of the most scenic and beautiful places. It is a popular tourist attraction in Trinidad. It is home to the Scarlet Ibis bird."

Hema interrupted, saying, "My dear sister, let me continue, please. Your turn will come."

"Let me speak please," Puja replied. Then she continued speaking to Moe. "I want to go to college here and further my studies—that is, when my dad can afford to send me."

Hema was quiet now, so Puja jumped into the conversation. She was most anxious to join in and contribute to the conversation. Puja started with a radiant smile, saying, "I attended a Hindu college in Trinidad. I love that school. My dad decided to come here, so I had to leave. I love to dance, and I want to continue that art form here."

Moe interjected, "That is all well and good, but children come here and get distracted with a lot of things. Be careful. Your formal education in school comes foremost in your life. Without your proper education, you are like a dog in the street, looking for its next meal. Your father is not rich, so you all have to be the best at what you do. Work towards scholarships for your higher education. We all are foreigners in this sacred land.Therefore, you have to work harder and more diligent than the citizens that are live here already."

Sandra said, "I would like to become a nurse. That requires a lot of time, effort and sacrifice. Time will tell what the future holds for me".

Moe added, laughing, "Where is poor Moonan going to get all this money to make sure your dreams are a reality? Education is the key to liberation from poverty. Without your formal education, you are nothing. Make the best of your time in school."

There was a deadly silence again. The sun was disappearing in the horizon. The rays of the sun looked beautiful as it tried to penetrate the darkened clouds. My father had told me that the sun is the centre of all life. Without the sun, there will be no life. The glimmer of the sun's rays reminded me that there was hope for tomorrow. Nature was at peace with itself in Naples. There was a feeling of tranquility in the air. The sun had disappeared into the distant sky. We were now in the beautiful Naples. Our lives had taken an unexpected turn, hopefully for the best circumstances.

It was pitch dark when we reached Moe's hotel. His family was anxiously awaiting his arrival. Moe smiled when he saw his family sitting on the veranda. His beautiful wife rushed to greet him with a kiss. Then she turned her attention to my family. She introduced herself and her three children, saying, "Hello, I am Sita. I am the wife of that handsome gentleman that brought you all from Miami. These are my three children. This is Robert and my two daughters, Kim and Joan."

Hema intervened and said, "Excuse me, it was a long ride. Can I use the restroom, please?"

"Yes," said Sita, realizing the urgency of the situation.

I think everyone was glad that Hema asked that question. Everyone rushed in the direction of the restroom, including Moe. After all, it was a long drive. Sita invited us to partake in a scrumptious dinner. It was a buffet with a variety of dishes. Everyone ate ravenously.

Hema and Puja sat on both sides of my chair. This was certainly our best meal in Florida. Dinner lasted about one hour.

Sandra complimented Sita for our fantastic meal. We helped dispose off the garbage and wash the dishes. Sita motioned us to their living room to have an acquaintance talk with a special God-sent family. She started the conversation with a pleasant smile. "We are Trinidadians to our heart and down to our bones, but we love United States foremost. This is my country, and I will die here. Moe has a fondness for helping people in distress. That is why my husband rushed to help you all without a second thought. In this world, people are engulfed in their problems, but we try to help when it is humanly possible. I am a Hindu, and Moe is a Muslim. We respect and love each other's values, culture, and religion."

Hema was quick to interject. "That is so nice to hear. My dad sent us to a Presbyterian School. There we learnt about Christian values and teachings, but we practice Hindu values and their way of life. I believe it gives a broad-spectrum view of life from every angle."

Moe quickly added, "Muslims are branded as one war-crazy people and are judged because of the fanatical and lunatic actions of a few people. God is great. Just have faith in him."

I could sense that philosophy came from within Moe's heart. For a split second, his jovial face changed to one of a serious nature. I think Moe was reminiscing of the attack of 9/11 when fanatics decimated the lives of thousands of innocent souls.

We sat silently as Moe spoke of this incident. Sensing the tenseness and uneasiness in the room, he changed the topic of discussion.

"Moonan, you love fishing. I heard the good news from your daughters. In the morning bright and early, we are going fishing for bass fish. When we return, we are going job-hunting for you. Hey, man, learn to relax and take it easy. God takes care of his people. Relax, you are in America. Get some rest because we leave early in the morning."

I was quick to add, "My friend, I was fishing since I was only five years. My father taught us the art of fishing early in life. Our fishing rods were from the bamboo trees that grew abundantly on the banks of the Caroni River. My first big catch was a six-pound tilapia. I was afraid to remove my catch from the hook because it looked so ugly. Anyway, we will continue talking in the morning. Goodnight and thank you."

Sita escorted us to our apartment. It was one room with three beds and a couch.

She said, "It is not the best, but you guys make the best of it. Try to make yourself comfortable. Have a good night's sleep. Moonan, do not worry, Moe will help you in any way possible."

I told her, "Sita, I deeply appreciate your help. You all came at the right time to my rescue. I would have been lost without your family's assistance. Thank you and goodnight.

How can we repay your family for all the inconveniences that we causing you".

Sita was laughing," Moonan, when we help you we get blessing and more prosperity for our family."

Sandra ensured that all the children were comfortable. Everyone was exhausted from our long trip. I could hear that familiar snoring sound coming from their beds. I had just dozed off when I heard a loud banging on the door. I pulled the curtain lazily to see who was knocking at this ungodly hour. It was a smiling Moe at the door.

"Good morning, my friend," he said. "This is the time to catch the biggest bass fish. Let us go quickly. I am giving you five minutes to get ready. I have already packed food, drinks, and all the fishing equipment. Please hurry up."

At this moment, I felt like telling Moe that I was totally exhausted.

When someone goes all the way to help you, should you be nice to them or you are biting the hand that is helping you? Moe was trying his utmost best to make me forget my immediate troubles. Therefore, I should cooperate in every way. I forgot my tiredness and jumped into his vehicle.

My family was fast asleep. Hema and Puja wanted to go fishing too, but they were exhausted.

The sun was already protruding its radiant head through the thick, dark clouds.

My father had said to me that all beautiful things of life are free. He was referring to the sun, the moon, and all of nature. We have to take time to absorb the goodness and exotic beauty that is free. Compared to the minute problems that we face in life, we must stop to observe nature in all her glory. I took a deep breath and said to myself, "I am going to enjoy this beautiful day."

I pondered about life, whether we should worry about situations that we have no control over.

Then I realized that all problems would be resolved in time. We may not like the outcome, but there is a result eventually, for better or for worse. Moe was unusually quiet that morning. I think he was tired from all his recent driving.

He never said anything about his tiredness. However, he looked as if he would fall asleep soon.

He drove carefully about three miles from his home. The countryside was breathtakingly beautiful. This area reminded me of the countryside in Trinidad. There were lush green fields and a wide array of multicolored trees. I saw a variety of birds. Nature was at peace with itself in Naples. Moe stopped at a secluded tranquil area to fish.

The area was well shaded from the sun. The trees were bent toward the water as though they were paying homage for providing water for their survival. Moe was happy to be there.

I think the area provided a refugee away from everyday problems. There was a special glow in his face. He said with reverence, "This is my fishing spot. No one knows about the large bass fish you catch here. This is my refugee from everything. I have caught the biggest bass right here."

I jokingly added, "Now I know, so this is my spot. I also know where to catch the biggest bass fish."

Within a few minutes, I felt a vigorous tug on my fishing rod. I jerked it quickly.

Suddenly, out of the water jumped the biggest bass fish I have ever seen in my life.

The fishhook was firmly embedded in the bass's mouth.

Moe said happily, "Stay with him. Do not let him get away. He is a big fella."

I handled the rod like a true professional. I had received my early training from my dad.

As the bass pulled the line, I held it steady. The natural instinct of the fish was to try to dislodge the hook from his mouth. From time to time, he jumped out the water, shaking his head vigorously.

Moe kept on shouting, "Stay with him! Stay with him! Do not let him go! Wow! He is a big boy. Stay with him. Moonan. Do not go near the water. Stay on the dry land. There are huge, vicious crocodiles lurking in the waters."

I was so focused on my prize that I did not realize that I was drifting toward the dangerous water. The commotion had attracted two large crocodiles. They had surfaced and were watching the action live as it happened. When the bass pulled, I reciprocated. We fought for about thirty minutes. Then I reeled him toward the shore. Two menacing-looking crocodiles in search of an easy meal followed him closely.

Moe shouted sternly to me, "When you go fishing in Florida, stay on the dry land! You could have been a meal today for crocs. This is their habitat. We can easily be their prey." Moe caught three more bass but not as big as my single catch. He taught me an important lesson that the hunter can become the hunted. "When you are in forested areas, do not focus on a single thing but observe everything around you." I was focused on my prized fish, but the crocodiles could have easily devoured me.

The sun was directly overhead as we proceeded to Moe's home. I had copied his mode of dressing. Today, I wore short pants and a light jersey. Our plans were to return home, clean the fishes, and barbeque them for lunch.

On reaching the hotel, my family was in the car park, playing cricket. This game is similar to baseball. It also is played with a bat and ball. It is popular in countries where Great Britain was their colonial master in the past. It is played regularly in Africa, India, Australia, Pakistan, Canada, England, West Indies, and Bangladesh. The sport is now gaining some recognition in the Western Hemisphere.

When we reached the parking lot, Hema and Puja rushed to the vehicle.

Hema said, "Daddy, how you can go fishing without us? You know we are your riding partners. You cannot go anywhere without us. Why you did not wake us up?"

I said, laughing, "Both of you were snoring loudly. You were dead asleep. Next time, we will certainly take both of you."

Hema and Puja had accompanied me on a lot of fishing trips in Trinidad. We had spent a lot of time fishing for tilapias, crabs, lobsters, and the ever-popular cascadura. They know the dangers and vicious nature of the alligators and crocodiles. Avoiding them is the essence of survival.

The American Dream

Moe gave us instructions on how and where to clean the fishes. He then departed to his office. We were hungry, so we hurriedly cleaned the fishes. We then seasoned the fishes and tossed them to the grill.

Mala was crying, so I held her, while my wife prepared her feeding bottle.

Puja said, "I think she was irritated and tired from all the traveling. Daddy, let me hold her. Maybe she will be quiet then."

Puja stretched out her hands to receive baby Mala who stopped crying in her sister's comforting hands.

Moe had disappeared for about an hour. We were focused on a hearty meal of fishes.

Moe reappeared when we had finished cooking. He was speaking to someone on the phone.

He said, "Moonan, this phone call is for you. One of my friends wants to speak to you about working in his pharmacy."

I hurriedly grabbed the phone. Jose, Moe's friend, was on the phone, and he introduced himself to me, saying, "I am Jose. I am the owner of Sunset Pharmacy. I am looking for a pharmacy intern urgently. You have to start in three days. If you accept this job, then you will have to come to

Miami. I will help you get an apartment in Miami. Moe told me all about your problems. He is my close friend, and I am trying to help a friend in every way. We have a pharmacy manager who will treat you very professionally. She is like a mother to me. We will file all the paperwork for you with the Pharmacy Board."

My heart skipped a beat. My hands felt as if I could touch the skies. This was mind-blowing news to me. This was like a bright shining light at the end of the tunnel.

Jose continued, "Come to Miami alone. You will find an apartment, then you can bring your family from Naples. I promise that I will work with you in every way to ensure you and your family are happy in Miami. Moe will make all the arrangements."

"Thank you again, sir. I appreciate your trust in me. I promise to do my best to make your business reach greater heights" was my energized response.

I rushed to Moe and hugged him with all my strength and said, "You are a true human being. You are a true friend. I am glad that I met you here. My family would have had to return to Trinidad without a job. I would have been at a loss without you. You and your family have showered unselfish kindness and love. We as a family will be eternally grateful. I will never forget your kindness."

Tears poured from my eyes.

I pondered about life for a minute. Is your life planned in advance, and we are just players in the game called life? Does it make sense worrying about situations that is beyond our control? For example, the problem regarding a work, would it be resolved in time? One thing, however, is that Moe was right on target. Everything always works for the best. We must have patience and the serenity to walk one step at a time.

I placed my hand on his shoulders and bowed to him, saying, "When one person disappointed me, I found refuge in you. You are my tower of strength. You were my savior in Florida. Thank you, sir. I humbly appreciate your kindness and generosity."

Both families were gathered to hear the good news. There were hugs and kisses for everyone.

I looked to the skies, and my heart was at peace with the world. Now I could eat a big hearty meal and relax with my new friends.

For the next two days, Moe requested my help around his hotel.

What is the concept of a living dead? That was the question. And how does it pertain our lives?

On my departure from Trinidad, my father said, "Do not be a living dead in America."

My father never received a formal education, but his philosophy was mind-boggling.

My brothers and sisters were awed by his high level of thinking and common sense application to life.

A living dead is a person who exists in this world only to help himself. The feelings of others are not important to him or her. That person uses someone as a stool or a stepping-stone for his or her personal advancement. That person is very pleasant and kind to others, but his or her motives are ulterior. That is why the world is upside down, people or topsy-turvy. A living dead walks and lives in every sector of our society. This exists in every race and religion. Mr. Pat from Hurts Rx Pharmacy is a good example of a living dead. Moe is not a living dead. Society benefits from the helpfulness of Moe and his family. Jesus Christ said, "Give unto others as I have given unto you" and "Love your neighbor as yourself."

To achieve peace in this world, we must be at peace with each other and ourselves. Then we will have no living dead in our utopic society.

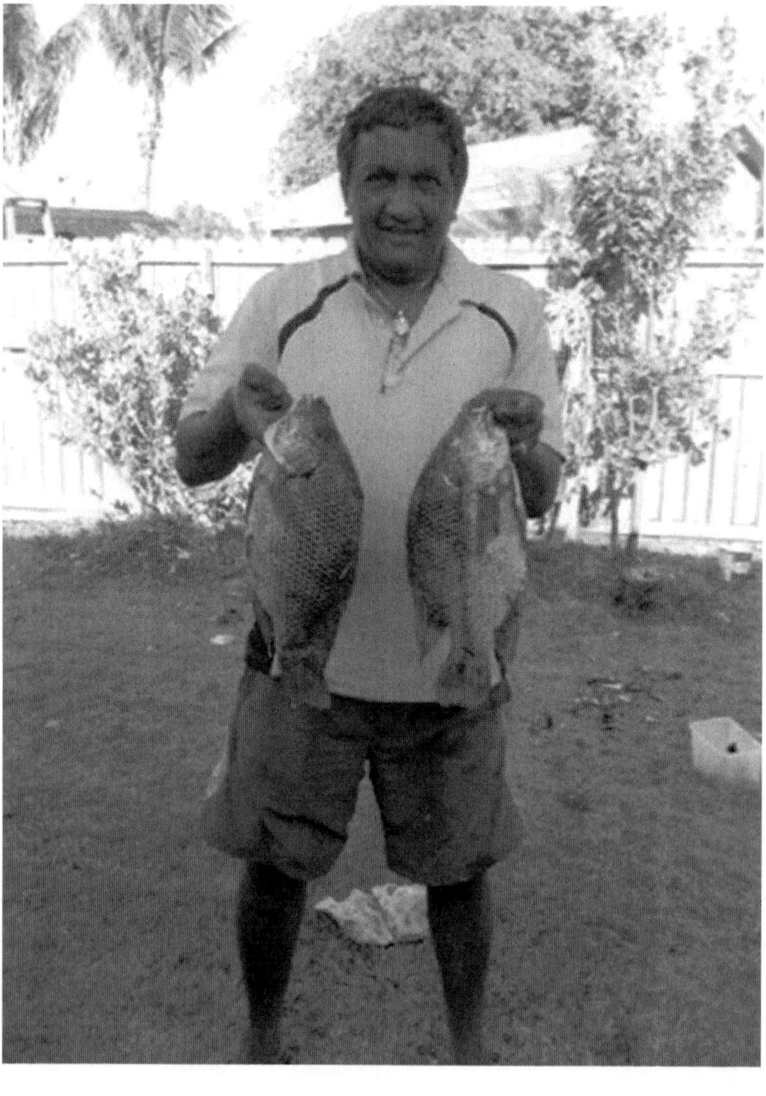

CHAPTER THREE

Good News: It Is Back to Miami

Our journey back to Miami began before the break of dawn. The previous night, I had a serious family discussion about the state of our dwindling finances. My message was simple: we needed to curtail our unnecessary spending to a minimum. On leaving the apartment, Hema and Puja could not understand why they could not accompany me to Miami. Hema pleaded, "Daddy, we will sleep on the floor. It is no problem for us. We want to go with you, please, please."

Hema was sincere in her desire to go to Miami. Tears were streaming down her eyes.

"I do not have any plans nor do I know what to expect. Do not worry. You will join me soon" was my simple reply.

Even my comforting embrace could not reassure Hema that this decision for her to stay in Punta Gorda was justified. Could I risk having my daughters with me in an uncertain situation? The drive to Miami was relaxing and enlightening. Just the mere knowledge that soon I was going to be gainfully employed made me very hopeful. It was another hot and sweltering day. As we drove, Moe offered me advice on everything, especially about working in Miami.

"In Miami, the culture is totally different. You are a stranger in a foreign land. Be careful. Stay away from lonely places. It is a vibrant place but just be careful of strangers."

He laughed heartily and joked about everything.

The short space of time that I spent with Moe taught me that he had many experiences about life. The knowledge that he shared with me was priceless.

On reaching the pharmacy, Jose was sitting outside on a bench. As we walked from the parking lot, Moe stopped me with this adamant advice, "Jose is going to offer you coffee. Make sure you drink it. Do not refuse the coffee. It is a tradition among Cubans to offer coffee as a way of welcoming their friends."

He then reiterated, "Just drink the damn coffee, please. Do not refuse. No excuses, please."

I added shyly, "I drank coffee a few times, and my stomach was on fire and then I developed diarrhea for a few days. To get this job, I will do what is necessary to get it."

Jose saw us coming to the pharmacy and rushed to hug his best friend, saying, "Hola, mi amigo, como esta?" (Or "Hello, my friend, how are you?")

Moe responded, "Todo bien, amigo." (Or "All is well, my friend.")

Jose continued, saying, "It is a long time I have not seen you. How are you and the family?"

Moe added with a broad smile, "All is well. I cannot complain. Life is good. My wife and I are busy with the hotel and my kids. You know how it is with kids. They keep you very occupied. Hey, man, this is Moonan. He is Dr. Ravi's friend from Trinidad."

Jose interrupted Moe, saying, "Let us go to the restaurant next door. I am hungry, and I need some coffee urgently. Then we can discuss work. You cannot talk about work on an empty stomach. Lunch is on me. I am paying for whatever you guys want to eat today."

Jose was about five feet in height, but he walked very fast to the restaurant.

He motioned for us to follow him. We reached a beautiful Spanish restaurant. Jose ordered three large cups of coffee for us.

Jose and Moe consumed the coffee with ease. I drank half a cup, and my stomach was on fire. I felt nauseous, but there was a smile on my face.

Jose looked at me and said, "The coffee is really good."

"This is the best coffee I have ever tasted in my lifetime. Wow, it's the best!" was my pleasant answer.

Jose summoned the waitress and said, "Mi amor, hello, can you bring a large cup of coffee for my friend? Thank you gracias."

I smiled wryly and said, "Thank you, this is just what I wanted—another bigger cup of coffee."

After hearing my remark, Moe looked at me very seriously.

Jose ordered a dish called paella from the menu. The food was made from a variety of seafoods and vegetables.

The food was tasty and mouthwatering. Jose spoke at length about his pharmacy. His goal was to make his customers happy.

He turned to me and said, "If you are committed to providing first-class professional care, then the job is yours."

"Sir, I owned and operated my pharmacy in Trinidad. There is only one type of service that is important and that

Journey of an Immigrant

is to treat customers like you. The secret to the successful business is customer satisfaction" was my zestful answer.

Jose laughed loudly. Everyone in the restaurant turned to look at him. He was not bothered by the constant stares from other patrons. He then said loudly, "My friend, the job is yours. Wow! I love your answer. Moe spoke highly of you, and that is enough for me. Moe is my friend. I love him like a brother, so his word is worth its weight in gold. You can start working from Monday morning at nine o'clock."

With that statement, Moe said good-bye. He was returning to Naples.

Jose said, "You can stay at Best Western Hotel tonight. Tomorrow morning, I will take you to look for an apartment that you can rent for your family. Do not worry about a thing. We will have your back covered."

Moe and Jose had one thing in common. Nothing in life seemed to be a problem. Moe's philosophy was that time resolves all issues. He said,

"Times are the master of your destiny. What you do with that precious time determines your character and your future".

Jose drove me in his Mercedes sports car to the Best Western Hotel. He was driving very fast and, at the same time, speaking on his cell phone. We reached the hotel in a few minutes.

"Thank you, sir, for giving me this opportunity to work in your pharmacy" was my humbly answer as I exited his posh luxury car.

"Remember, Moonan, tomorrow we are going to look for an apartment. Adios. Be prepared to move quickly."

With that statement, Jose sped quickly away.

The two large cups of coffee had a nauseating effect on my stomach. My first stop was to the restroom. My stomach was on fire. I knew that feeling would remain throughout the night.

After checking into the hotel, I returned to the lobby to make a long delayed telephone call to Trinidad. Since my arrival in Florida, I did not speak to anyone in Trinidad. Now, there was some positive light on my employment.

This was good news and a positive reason to call my loved ones.

My son, Jewan, answered the telephone.

My voice was full of exuberance and excitement. Jewan was always on my mind.

There was a vacuum created inside me by my absence from Trinidad. When I heard his voice, I felt the emptiness gone. There was excitement in my voice.

"Son, how are you? My goodness, I miss you much. How are your studies coming along? Is everything all right?" I asked a few questions before Jewan could say a word. "Please focus on your studies. You cannot afford to repeat any courses." I was shooting many questions to my son because the phone card had only ten minutes usage. Finally, I allowed my son to speak.

"Daddy, I really missed you. Life is not the same without you. I am trying to focus and get on with my life, especially my university studies. I will be all right. Grandpa and Grandma help me a lot. I will be okay, but please keep in touch."

His voice was sad and sorrowful. Tears filled my eyes. It was difficult for him, but I knew that he is strong. I knew that he can cope with any problems that comes his way. Jewan wanted me to say hello to my father and mother because the minutes in my phone card were been quickly depleted. I heard, "You have one minute remaining."

My father came on the telephone. "Dad, how are you? Everything is fine. I am working. I love you all. Say hello to all my family."

Then the telephone was disconnected. My phone card was depleted. All the minutes were utilized.

After a long and exhausting day, my mind was at ease. I slept like a baby, knowing my job was secured with Sunset Pharmacy. My stomach was still on fire from my encounter with the coffee, but that was of no consequence.

Sunday morning at eleven o'clock, Jose was waiting for me in the hotel lobby.

He gave me a big hug and said, "Buenos dias amigo, como estas?" (Meaning, "Good morning, how are you?") "I brought you a large cup of coffee like the one you enjoyed in the restaurant."

He was pleasantly surprised when I answered, "Todo bien y tu?" (Meaning, "I am good and you?")

Now, he said, "Drink your coffee, and let us go apartment-hunting."

He looked at me as if he was supervising my drinking of the coffee. According to Moe, "Do not refuse his hospitality."

Suddenly, Jose's cell phone rang, and he exited the hotel lobby to get some privacy. Here was an opportunity to dispose off the coffee in a potted plant in the hotel lobby.

Jose returned after a few minutes. He was surprised that I had drunk all the coffee so quickly.

Now, our task was to get an apartment near the pharmacy. This would make it easier to access to and from work at the pharmacy.

As we drove on our mission, it was necessary to tell Jose about my limited finances.

"Jose, I do not have a lot of money at this time. I do not want a fancy or expensive apartment. Maybe a two-bedroom with a kitchen."

He was deep in thought and said, "I spoke to my wife. She said that no one would rent an apartment to you. They will require seeing your legal documents for Florida. They will check on your credit, but you have none here. This is what I am going to do for you. I am going to take the apartment in my name. Then I am going to pay the deposit or security. Every month, I will subtract from your salary the money that I paid. Now, I am taking this risk because of Moe and Ravi."

I could not believe what I was hearing.

I told Jose, "I am lucky to have found helpful people like Moe and you in Florida. Without you people, I would have been at a loss or would have had to return to Trinidad.

Thank you. I promise you that I will work diligently and honestly in your pharmacy."

Jose signed the lease for the apartment. He gave me the keys for the apartment. The apartment was located about three miles from the pharmacy.

Jose gave me his pharmacy call card with the pharmacy address.

With these departing words, he left, "Please be on time for work at nine in the morning. Punctuality is something I love to see in my staff. Do not be late. You are on your own, Brother. See you tomorrow, *adios*."

I called Moe on the phone to inform him of the latest developments.

No mention was made to him about the lease agreement. I was too embarrassed to discuss the goodness and generosity of his friend.

Moe was happy for me, and he added, "On Saturday, I will bring your family back to Miami. They are enjoying themselves. They are out shopping with my wife. You have to show Jose that you are a diligent and a dedicated worker. This will be my reward, knowing that Jose has a good impression of you. Make me proud."

My answer to Moe was very reassuring. "Do not worry about me. I will show Jose how to improve his pharmacy. After all, I owned and operated two pharmacies in Trinidad."

With that final word, the phone was disconnected. I redialed, but the phone card had no remaining minutes.

It was three o'clock in the afternoon. It was another blistering hot day. I decided to get acquainted with my immediate surroundings.

Armed with a pen and a notebook, I started discovering my neighborhood. There was a shopping plaza about half a mile away, so I walked in that direction. At the plaza, most of the people could not speak English. My Middle Eastern countenance attracted a lot of attention.

People stared at me with concern and curiosity. Their concern, to some extent, was justified; the effects of 9/11 were a reality. However, I am a third-generation East Indian, yet people looked at me in fear and suspicion.

My father had said, "Words do not kill. Do not get into conflict because of a foul mouth or racial person. You are born a certain race. Be proud and walk tall among people. Live a peaceful life. But do not mistake meekness for weakness."

I could feel many eyes piercing my body as I surveyed the surrounding neighborhood. This was not a major concern.

It was a cool sunny evening; nature was complimenting my mood.

There was a sense of relief inside me that my God was protecting me. The birds were chirping in the trees. Even the evening sun was smiling with its brilliant sunlight, and I said, "Thank you, God, for taking care of me."

At a nearby pharmacy, I purchased an inflatable bed.

The cashier told me, "Senor, treinta pesos."

I was confused and said, "Treinta pesos, but do you accept American money?"

Her supervisor stepped forward because the line at the register was now getting longer.

"What she means is thirty American dollars."

My next stop was at the supermarket. Again, no one spoke a word of English.

Was it different strokes for different folks? As a prerequisite for my pharmacy qualifications, I had to write three English examinations even though I came from an

English-speaking country. My next stop was at the gas station. The attendant's accent was surely Middle Eastern.

His English was extremely broken. He was relieved to see someone that looked like him.

He asked, "My friend, what part of Pakistan is you from? My name is Samir. I am from Karachi."

Smiling, I answered, "Hello, my name is Moonan, How are you? No, I am from Trinidad in the West Indies."

He was surprised when I told him that I was not from Pakistan. Like myself, the culture and language was different, but it takes time to acclimatize to a foreign land. I purchased my phone card and left the gas station.

"Thank you very much. See you again, Samir."

I laughed heartily to myself as I departed from the gas station. Does everyone believes someone that looks Middle Eastern comes only from Pakistan?

Then it dawned on me that Samir was lonely and isolated in a foreign culture. No one understood his way of life or was too ignorant to learn to enlighten their life.

My shopping cart, which was full of items, needed refrigeration. It was important to reach the apartment urgently. I thought maybe Samir would be my friend one day.

Personality, not appearance, is a better judge of character. Racial profiling is a common factor among people. We judge the whole race of people by the fanatical actions of a few people. Racial profiling is a dangerous precedent. In every culture or race, there are good and bad people.We have to reach out and find them.

On reaching my apartment, my body was tired. My inflatable bed was a welcome companion.

I fell into a deep tranquil sleep.

Bernard Shaw said, "Life is not about finding yourself. It is about creating yourself."

Creating a new life in Florida would start from this empty apartment. It would take courage and fortitude to reach that goal.

The beautiful scintillating chirping sounds of a cockatiel awoke me. He was sitting outside on the apartment porch. His body was pure white with red eyes. This majestic bird danced from side to side, singing the most melodious songs. It brought a smile to my face.

Any sign of loneliness or anxiety that existed within me earlier had disappeared with his chirping sounds.

Nature was welcoming me to Miami in a grand fashion.

CHAPTER FOUR

My Pharmacy Training Begins

A new chapter in my life had begun. It is the dawn of a new beginning. It was a three-mile trek to Sunset Pharmacy. Jose had previously given me the directions to his pharmacy. It was a cool Monday morning. It was ideal weather for walking.

There was a lot of traffic pileup at seven o'clock in the morning. I was focused on reaching early to the pharmacy. I wanted to create a good impression on my first day to work in Miami. Besides, Jose had given me a stern but gentle warning about latecoming. My long legs were being stretched to the limit.

My mind traveled back to Trinidad as I continued my journey toward the pharmacy.

In my country, I owned and operated two pharmacies. Baijoo Drugstore and SMD Pharmacy were household names. Both were very popular, and customers loved the friendly and professional services.

The American Dream

Every customer was treated as if they were a special person. Thousands of customers loved the products that we manufactured for sale. My very own line of products like hair food, ointments for pain, and chest rubs were fast movers. My sister, Mena, was the manager of the pharmacy.

My love for helping people was the passion of my life. However, after two robberies at my pharmacies, my desire to own pharmacies or live in my beloved Trinidad had vanished. The last robbery was very traumatic.

Two armed bandits held up the pharmacy at gunpoint when Hema, Puja, and I were in the pharmacy. In that incident, one of the bandits placed the gun inside my mouth and threatened to pull the trigger.

The only consolation that the police gave me after the investigation were, "Thank God that you are still alive."

The honking of car horns on Eighth Street shook me back to reality. Now that I was an employee and not an employer, how was I to cope with the reverse roles?

I felt energized and confident that I made the right decision to migrate to America.

Trinidad is in the past. Florida is now the land of my dreams.

I have confronted death numerous times in my life.

Nothing is more gruesome than a bandit brandishing a gun at you and your employees, threatening to kill everyone. In life, you have to be realistic and say enough is enough.

After walking steadily for one-and-a-half hours, I finally reached Sunset Pharmacy. I was sweating profusely by that time.

My finances were dwindling very rapidly. Therefore, I needed a source of income. My mode of dress was immaculate. The feeling of employment had my body energized and focused to work.

Jose was waiting outside the pharmacy. He was sitting on the bench, accompanied by two large cups of coffee at his side. His love for Cuban cafe was overwhelming.

Jose reached up, hugged me, and said, "Hola amigo, como estas?" (Meaning, "Good morning, how are you?") "Here is your hot morning coffee. Drink and enjoy before you start to work. Relax for now, as we still have a few minutes before opening time."

Jose looked at me, ensuring that not even a drop of coffee was wasted.

One question came to my mind: Was their toilet in working condition?

We relaxed and drank coffee. It was time to start working. When Jose opened the pharmacy door, there was a simultaneous shout of "Welcome (or *Bienveniedios*)" from his seventeen employees. Jose and his staff had planned a surprise welcome for me. I was elated that his staff had planned a welcome party with food and drinks. Jose introduced his staff individually.

The last person that he introduced was Dr. Maria, my new pharmacy supervisor.

She was a petite lady with a natural radiant smile. She welcomed me with a hug, a kiss, and of course, a large cup of coffee. Dr. Maria was of Cuban descent.

Today was my lucky day for coffee. Everyone asked about Dr. Ravi from Trinidad. "When is Dr. Ravi coming back to Miami? Is he all right? Is he married now? Does he have a girlfriend?."

Dr. Ravi had made a big impact on Sunset Pharmacy. With his expertise and guidance, the pharmacy had reached new heights of success. Everyone admired him. Replacing their beloved, Dr. Ravi proved to be a daunting task. However, my ambition was to exceed their expectations. I wanted to prove that I could help carry this pharmacy to new heights.

"Moonan," Dr. Maria said, "let us submit your paperwork to the Pharmacy Board at once. I want to ensure that you do not encounter any problems. Give me all the relevant documents. I am going to fax everything right now. Today, we have many medications to dispense for retirement and assisted living facility homes. All these have to be delivered by eleven o'clock tonight, or we will lose our contract. We have lost two contracts in the past month. We cannot afford that to happen again."

Her faced changed to a serious and concerned look as she continued to speak, saying, "When we lose a contract to supply a home with medications, we lose a lot of money. Then we have to lay off experienced and dedicated workers. Jose hired you to ensure this does not happen again. You speak English fluently, which is an asset. Most of his workers only speak Spanish. That is a big problem here. I want you to supervise and rectify any problems that we encounter with the homes."

"When a problem arises, call the managers of the homes."

"Dr. Maria," I said, "just show me what is required, and I will work on it speedily and efficiently."

We worked feverishly as a well-coordinated team to meet the deadline. There were hardly any communication between the workers. Everyone knew that there were deadlines to meet and worked feverishly to accomplish their individual task. Coffee was served regularly. Boxes after boxes of medications were completed and labeled for delivery. Everything was verified and rechecked under the watchful eyes of Dr. Maria. The staff was prepared to work late hours. Everyone had brought their sweaters and extra food. I wanted to create a good impression, so my mind was very focused on my allocated work.

It is not a good idea on your first day on a new job to make any mistakes.

Suddenly, there was a burning sensation on my right shoulder. It was Jose trying to lighten the mood. He slammed his robust right hand on my back.

"What's up, Brother? Today, we have to finish all the work. Please stay until all the work is completed. Thank you, my brother."

With that dramatic entrance, he exited the pharmacy with his cell phone to his ears.

Jose's staff was happy. They smiled when I passed their workstation. We finished at midnight. I was glad and relieved that I had completed my first day at work. There was a feeling of satisfaction that I was now working in an

American pharmacy. I said, "Buenas noches." (Meaning, "Good night.")

I then began my journey homewards to my apartment. My love for the pharmacy profession was unchanged. My love for hard work was unchanged. On reaching the street on my journey to my apartment, I remembered a quotation from Kahlil Gibran: "Work is love made visible. If you cannot work with love but only with distaste, then it is better that you leave your work and sit at the temple and take offering from people who work with joy and love."

Outside the pharmacy, it was pitch black. The streets were deserted. There was hardly any vehicle on the streets. The night was still and quiet. I felt afraid and all alone. My plan was to run as fast as my lanky long legs could take me.

There were some menacing dark clouds hanging in the overhead skies. In the distant skies, there was a rapid outburst of thunder and lightning. Every minute, the sounds and flashes of thunder and lightning grew nearer to my location. I felt isolated and trapped in the darkness. Florida is known as the lightning capital of the world.

Every year, many people are killed by lightning in this state. This horrendous fact pierced my frightened mind. My long legs were being stretched to the limit of my endurance.

The heavy downpour was now directly overhead. Within a few minutes, my clothes were totally drenched from the heavy downpour. The intermittent outburst of thunder was like a sonic boom. It sent shivers into my trembling body.

The quick succession of lightning that followed lit up the dark skies. I could feel that death's door was opening. The usually heavy downpour caused the streets to flood quickly. In the darkness of the night, pairs of fluorescent eyes were seen swimming in the waters. I screamed out loud, but I was all alone at the mercy and fury of Mother Nature. The lightning had struck a large tree, and it fell onto the pavement. My best choice was to maneuver onto the street to bypass this obstacle.

The tall palm trees were swaying helplessly in the wind. I told myself jokingly that this was my baptism on my first working day in America. Nothing was going to deter my goal in qualifying as a pharmacist.

I reached my apartment unharmed but traumatized by this unexpected incident. In my bathroom, my mind was trying to digest what had transpired that night.

I showered and retired to the safety of my inflatable bed. In a few hours, the melodious songs of my feathered friend awoke me from my tranquil sleep. My cockatiel friend had returned to give some of his heavenly melodies.

His haunting music lasted about ten minutes. To show my appreciation for his scintillating performance, I placed bread on a plate on the porch. I hoped he liked bread.

On my way to work in the morning, my first stop was McDonald's. I wanted to look at their breakfast menu.

Every item on their menu was a meat product. It is difficult to get vegetarian food here. I missed my traditional breakfast in Trinidad. It is normally vegetarian in the morning. A typical breakfast consisted of roti or bread with a variety of beans, eggplant, or potatoes. Meat is normally not served for breakfast. I walked briskly toward Sunset Pharmacy. I was tired and hungry. My stomach was still on fire, so I moved swiftly toward my workplace. I wondered whether people migrating to America had similar experiences. Adaptation is the key to survival. Changes are inevitable if you have to survive in any new society.

James Harvey Johnson said, "Man is a product of nature, a part of the Universe. The Universe is operated under exact natural laws."

Man is a product of millions of years of evolution.

He adapts himself to the laws of nature, or else, he perishes.

On reaching the pharmacy, I greeted everyone with *Buenos dias* and *como estas*.

My father said, "Greet everyone according to their culture. It shows respect for their culture. It also shows your humility."

What my father meant was, "When you are in Rome, do like the Romans."

Greeting shows respect for someone's culture. For example, you will greet a Christian person "good morning," a Hindu person "namaste," and a Muslim person "Assalamu alaikum." This shows respect and love for the person's culture. Love and respect for someone's culture is very important to coexist in any country.

Dr. Maria summoned me to her office for a long discussion with her. My mind was worried.

Did I make mistakes on my first day on the job? Was my performance not up to their high standards? Dr. Maria said with a calming motherly smile on her face, "Moonan, please ensure that all your Pharmacy Board assignments are completed on time. I need to sign them as your supervisor and return them to the Board. This is mandatory. You also have to work training hours for about three months. Do not worry, time flies when you are enjoying your work. You remind me a lot of Dr. Ravi. I love your passion for working. You will make a very dedicated pharmacist. Just keep on trucking. Your priority presently is to pass the Board examination. It is a tough examination. Please focus on passing both exams. If you want help, I am here for you. Do not waste time going sightseeing and to casinos. All those things are irrelevant right now."

"Okay, Doctor," I said. "I am going to focus and pass the examination. I will definitely need your help."

She continued, "Dr. Ravi introduced me to East Indian food, and I cannot get enough of it. The taste is exotic. I love it. Can you make roti? I love roti. You know, I have visited India on many occasions. I love your music, culture, and language. I believe in the science of reincarnation. It is a science, not a myth. Dr. Ravi was very dedicated to the pharmacy profession. You are like him in many respects."

A smile lit up my face. "Doctor, when we settle in our apartment, I will cook a lot of Eastern Indian food for you. You can visit our apartment for dinner also."

She added, "Remember, life is a marathon, not a one-hundred-meter race. To succeed, you must be fast and steady. Make me proud of your achievements because I am your mentor and preceptor."

It was my second day in the pharmacy. I was flabbergasted. It blew my mind to think that someone cared and loved me so much professionally.

Dr. Maria was truly not a living dead that my father spoke about on my departure from Trinidad. The pharmacy was very busy. There was so much to learn about their system, procedures, and protocols. After my second day at the pharmacy, there was contentment in my heart. My walk to the apartment was brisk. Today, the skies were clear. On my way, I stopped at a Dollar store to purchase another phone card. The sales clerk asked me, "Are you from Pakistan?"

This time, I smiled and moved onto the apartment.

What was the obsession about Pakistan? This question pondered in my mind.

My primary intention was to speak to my son.

The telephone line was busy. My walking speed was getting faster and steadier.

I think my legs were adapting to my long walks. Maybe they were very numb from my long journey to and from the pharmacy. It was time to find solace and comfort in my inflatable bed.

My body was dehydrated. The coffee gave me diarrhea throughout the day. My body was beyond the stage of exhaustion. I fell into a deep sleep with a heavy examination book on top of my chest. My bed was strategically placed to listen to my melodious friend in the morning.

At promptly six in the morning, my feathered friend came to serenade me. What a wonderful way to wake up! It was natural and majestic music to my ears. This serenading would continue for two consecutive mornings. Moe had called Sunset Pharmacy to ensure that on Saturday morning, I would be at my apartment. He was planning to bring back my family from Naples. My family was looking forward to be reunited again.

CHAPTER FIVE

Disaster Strikes Hard

Saturday morning was unusually hot and humid. It was sweltering hot. It was unusual that there were no birds chirping in the trees. My friend, the cockatiel, did not wake me up with its melodious sounds. The day was unusually calm. The wind was still, and there was calmness in the air.

Moe was in Miami two hours earlier than his schedule visit. I thanked him for all the kindness he had showered on my family. Hema and Puja ran and hugged me tightly. Their eyes were filled with tears.

"I missed you, Daddy," both said simultaneously.

Sandra brought baby Mala for a special hug. Moe called me aside and said, "Hey brother, I have to go back home in a hurry."

I interrupted his conversation, saying, "Can you please take me to Goodwill Store? We have no beds for my family."

He hesitated but agreed to take me.

Moe agreed, but his mind was preoccupied, and he looked very unhappy. We raced quickly to the Goodwill Store.

In the store, Moe gave me some consoling words, "Do not worry, you are a typical immigrant. When I came here, my family had nothing. You are a typical immigrant trying to survive. You must creep before you start walking."

We purchased two beds and hurried back to the apartment. Moe helped me unload the unassembled beds and then turned to me and said in a serious tone, "My wife said to give you this small television. You have to carry the beds upstairs by yourself. I have to leave immediately."

He gave me a big hug and then sped away. Hema and Puja came back to help me.

We took everything upstairs and assembled the beds. I told Sandra to listen to the news on the television because the weather outside was unusually calm.

After a few minutes, she came running and said, "Moonan, come and see the news. Hurry up! According to the weather report, Naples is in the direct path of a major hurricane."

From my calculation, Moe was still traveling on the road to Naples. The safety of my newfound friend was weighing heavily on my mind.

Good friends are like diamonds; they are extremely rare gems. Using the phone in the lobby, I called Moe to inquire about his safety. There was no answer even after redialing. I was extremely worried about my friend.

God will surely protect his family against any danger, I thought. I rushed back to my apartment. My family sat glued to our small newly acquired television.

The hurricane was battering Naples. It had maximum sustained winds of 145 mph with punishing gusts of up to 175 mph. Its wind gust was capped at a ferocious and devastating 200 mph. We were grief-stricken for our newfound family. The hurricane remained over Naples for roughly four hours. It left an epic trail of devastation. Reports from the media were not encouraging. The area suffered widespread damage to both life and property. The surrounding areas of Naples also suffered a direct hit from the hurricane. Mobile homes were flattened or relocated by the hurricane. The roads were impassable because trees had fallen and blocked the roadway. The heavy rains brought excessive flooding. The drainage system could not cope with the massive amounts of rainfall occurring in a short space of time. The rivers burst their banks, unable to accommodate the excessive amounts of water.

The raging floods destroyed farmlands and drowned numerous animals. It was a common sight to see crocodiles or snakes crossing the roadways. There were fifteen-foot-high waves as the hurricane surged inland. Homes in the shorelines were decimated.

The Federal Government responded immediately and set up shelters for the thousands affected by the monster hurricane. I returned a few times throughout the night to call Moe on the telephone. There was no answer on the telephone. The telephone lines were dead.

My family was traumatized. We spoke throughout the night about Moe's kindness and generosity. I said to my family, "Life is uncertain. We do not know what tomorrow will bring. Then we need to appreciate the little that we have now. We should thank God for bringing us to America and finding good friends."

Hema and Puja liked my philosophy, so I continued, "There is no tomorrow. When tomorrow comes, it is today. Gandhi said 'Live everyday like it is your last day, but plan everyday like it is your first day'. Life changes with the blink of an eye, for better or for worse. So we have to enjoy every moment of life."

"Wow!" said Hema. "You are so right. I am tired. I am going to bed."

Everyone was tired. It was bedtime. Outside my apartment, it was a hot and humid night. The trees were bending continuously as strong winds battered them. The winds howled against the apartment windows. From time to time, there was a dazzling display of lightning followed by a deadly outburst of thunder. I felt that Mother Nature was furious with Florida. My family was tired; that familiar snoring sound was overwhelming. I fell asleep in my comfortable inflatable bed. My alarm awoke me up at seven o'clock. I looked frantically outside to see my cockatiel friend, but he was not there. I missed his melodious sounds in the morning. There was his food on the porch but no grand appearance.

Was it possible that my feathered friend had foreseen the impending disaster?

He must have been seeking refuge in a safe place before Mother Nature unleashed her fury.

Puja had said jovially about the bird, "Daddy, maybe God sent an angel to look after you in your times of loneliness. Someone to make you happy when I was not with you."

Did Puja believe that I had an imaginary friend?

It was Sunday morning. There was only dreadful news coming out of Naples. We stayed indoors because it was raining throughout the day.

Two weeks had gone by, and there was not a word from Moe and his family.

A feeling of helplessness crept over me.

Surely, if I had access to a vehicle then, I would have driven up to Naples.

Hiring a taxi was out of the question. The journey was only three hundred miles away. I felt helpless and depressed. Listening to the television was more depressing.

They said the roads to Naples were impassable.

The telephone lines were damaged beyond repair. Rescue efforts were coming from other states quickly to meet the desperate conditions. I could not focus on my studies.

Sometimes, I would look at the darkness of the night and try to paint an image of the living conditions in Naples after the hurricane: a place where there is no lights, little food, damaged homes, and hardly communications with the outside world.

I knew that Moe would say, "Be strong and fight a good fight to the finish. Never give up because life goes on regardless of the circumstances."

The rains had disappeared overnight. It was a cloudless Monday morning as I walked toward the pharmacy.

That day marked my fourteen days of working at Sunset Pharmacy. That means, I should have been paid already. I was panicking because I had only four hundred dollars remaining from the money that I brought from Trinidad. My funds were low. Now I was getting desperate with the situation.

At the pharmacy, I spoke to Jose, and he said, "My friend, I forgot to tell you that the first week salary is normally held as a security here. You will be paid on Friday or tomorrow."

At my apartment, my family discussed spending again. "Guys, we cannot afford to spend money on nonessential items like clothes or jewelry. We have no money except for foodstuffs."

Sandra, my wife, interrupted, saying, "How are we supposed to enjoy ourselves? This is America. Shopping is a woman's paradise here."

"For the present time, go and relax in the parks or join the library. We must sacrifice to achieve our dreams in this beautiful land. I have not received my salary yet for working in the pharmacy. If we continue spending, we will be broke soon" was my response.

I continued, "My dear Sandra, How much money do you have remaining from that money I gave you in Naples?"

Sandra was visibly upset at my question, and she said, "We spent them all on shopping for clothes and gifts. When I heard that you got the job, we went crazy shopping."

My facial expression changed to a serious countenance, and I said, "Yes, I have a job but no salary to this day. Anyway, we cannot spend what we do not have. As a mom, you have to restrain yourself from extravagant spending for the next few months."

Hema and Puja were more understanding than their mother about sacrifice and spending.

Friday morning was here. I ran to the pharmacy as briskly as my long legs could take me. This was a grand occasion to receive my first paycheck in the United States of America.

This was my special day. Jose brought the check and said, "I am glad you are here. You are now an asset to this company. Thank you for the wonderful work that you are doing. Dr. Maria speaks highly of you. Since you are here, we have not lost any contracts. Thank you, *amigo*."

I told him, "Boss, I need some time off from work to cash this check. Please, can I leave about forty-five minutes earlier?"

He paused and answered, "That is no problem. Clock out when you are leaving. Remember, when you clock out, you only get paid for the hours you have worked."

With my cherished check in my hand, I rushed out of the pharmacy in the direction of the bank. My legs were getting stronger from my constant walking with every passing day. The bank was about to close. With a broad confident smile, I approached the teller and said, "Hello, how are you? I came to cash a check, please."

She bluntly said, "If you do not have an account in this bank, you cannot cash a check."

She threw the check back on the counter and summoned the next customer in line.

I was flabbergasted. I called Jose from a pay phone, but there was no answer. This was a big disappointment. I felt like shouting and screaming from the top of my voice. I felt as if I was fighting the world. Nothing seemed to be working in my favor. Coming to America was a privilege and honor, but nothing seemed to be working in my favor. At my apartment, I explained to my family as to what had transpired.

My wife Sandra was not pleased. "It is simple. Just call your family in Trinidad. They will lend you some money."

"No," I said blatantly, "if you want to ask your family, that is fine. I am not going to call Trinidad and beg for money."

My wife replied, "We need money to shop. There is so much sale all over the mall."

My wife could not add any comforting words, but she just added fuel to a burning fire. To avoid any unnecessary argument, I stormed out of the apartment, very visibly upset. Life was becoming a big struggle. Nothing was working out correctly. Looking at the water fountain in the lobby of the hotel relaxed my troubled mind. Life was becoming difficult to understand but to migrate without money and friends made it impossible. There were so many obstacles on my way to success. Every path taken seemed to bring more distress. Within my family, a storm was brewing despite trying to satisfy all their needs. Hema and Puja came looking for me.

They both sat beside me and hugged me tightly. They are heaven-sent blessing. They are the jewels in the crown of my life. My mother always said, "My children are my crown jewels. They are my most precious possessions. The love I have for them makes them my crown jewels."

The phrase "crown jewel" was coined by the English to describe India.

Great Britain called India the jewel of the crown because it was the most valuable and precious colony. India provided for Britain an abundance of tea, cotton, spices, precious metals, and minerals. India had a large population, which also meant free or low-cost labor. From India, England was able to expand its influences and domination to China and the Far East. Now like my mother, I can say my children are my crown jewels.

My mind was confused. Was it better to strive, make yourself stronger, and be independent, or just be weak and accept help or beg for help?

Was I too arrogant to call Trinidad for help or just embarrassed to ask for money? I decided to sacrifice, spend less, and wait for my check to be processed.

The weekend passed uneventfully. On Monday morning, I rushed to Sunset Pharmacy.

"Jose, please help me resolve this issue. The bank would not cash the check without an American identification. I need this money desperately."

Jose added, "Hey, man, you have to go and get a Florida Identification card for you and the wife. Then you can go to the bank and open a bank account. You have to open a joint account so your wife can do all transactions in your absence."

Next morning, my wife and I were at the license office. The line was long, and it meandered outside the office. We waited about two hours, and then our turn came to speak to an African-American attendant.

JOURNEY OF AN IMMIGRANT

She said, "You have to make an appointment online on your computer. On that day, you can return with all the relevant documents. However, you can wait at the end of the day when all appointments are finished. Then we will help you."

I assured her that we had no choice but to wait. "Okay, we will wait. I do not have access to a computer nor do I own a computer. Please help us as early as possible. I am new to this country, and I desperately need an identification card to open a bank account. Please I will humbly appreciate your help."

She smiled and said, "Sir, everyone has a different problem and need my immediate attention. On the other hand, you can wait until all our appointments are completed throughout the evening. Then I can help you but that be a long wait."

She patiently returned three hours later. The actual processing of the application was very rapid. We were fortunate to see the same pleasant attendant.

After the process was completed, she said, "Thank you. You should receive the Florida Identification card in the mail within fourteen business days."

I pleaded to her and said, "Miss, I desperately need it today."

She impatiently added, "Sir, I do not make the rules. I simply follow them. Do not kill the messenger."

With a half smile, I said, "Thank you for all your help."

Now, Sandra and I rushed to Sunset Pharmacy to speak to Jose.

On reaching the pharmacy, I explained my dilemma to him, and he said, "I have five hundred dollars in cash. Please take this money now, and tomorrow, I will give you the rest in cash."

We thanked Jose for his help and started our journey toward the apartment.

It was a hot sweltering afternoon. This was a good opportunity for my wife to enjoy the conditions that I encountered daily. It was a time for my wife to enjoy a nice brisk walk. After about a mile, she complained, "Please call a taxi. I am extremely tired. I cannot go any further."

I said, "I do not have a cell phone. How are we going to call? Do not worry, it is not far again to the apartment."

She was not happy with my answer. We moved slowly onward. After another mile of walking, she said, "You walk this distance twice daily and you never complained to us."

I said philosophically, "Complaining is never going to resolve any issue. I do not want my children to worry about their father."

The afternoon skies were changing. The darkened clouds were looking menacing. The sun was overshadowed by the dark gray clouds. Thunder and lightning followed in rapid succession.

We were terrified. The showers of blessing came fast and without warning. My wife asked, "What should I do?"

I said frantically, "Run, run, run!"

The rain was continuous until we reached the apartment. We were drenched.

This was a good experience for my wife to understand the simple philosophy, "You have to creep before you can walk."

Hema and Puja were laughing at the ordeal. Their mother did not see the humor in this incident. Nelson Mandela said, "The greatest glory in living lies not in never failing, but in rising every time we fail."

Failure is part of living, but we must rise every time we fall. Never give up; pursue the fight for survival unrelentlessly. Failure depends on your weakness. Conquer failure and the world is yours.

CHAPTER SIX

Education Is the Key to Your Salvation and Liberation

Books are lighthouses erected in the sea of time. Previous generations have left us a legacy of knowledge. It is important that we absorb that knowledge and prevent ourselves from making the same mistakes. Knowledge is power. Knowledge is wealth to the mind, body, and spirit. Therefore, the education of my children was foremost in my mind. To reach the American dream, their education was the cornerstone to their success in America. My next step was to get my girls back into suitable schools.

There is a saying, "An idle mind is the devil's workshop."

Staying at home was not an option for them. In Trinidad, Hema had already graduated from high school. I wanted to wait until I obtained my pharmacist license, then send her to college. Now, my bills were higher than my monetary income. However, Puja's education was more important. In Trinidad, Puja was a very brilliant student in high school. She was an honor student. However, she did not finish her high school training. It was necessary to get her into high school immediately. Previously, I had faxed all the information to the principal from a nearby school. An appointment was necessary to see him. He was a very pleasant gentleman.

He was glad that we had chosen his school to further Puja's education.

He welcomed us warmly.

He said, "Puja's grades are fantastic, but we have to give her an entry-level examination. This will determine her placement class. I have arranged for her to write the exam today. Is she prepared to write the exam? You will notice our students are of diverse background here. It is a pleasure to have Puja at my school."

Puja was smiling. "Daddy, I was born ready." Her face was radiating with confidence.

The principal escorted Puja to the examination room.

Puja has always been a child with a beautiful smile and a brilliant mind.

In Trinidad, her teacher told me, "Moonan, I have only one problem with your daughter Puja. She is very talkative. Her mouth is never tired. She can join a conversation on any topic and talk all the time. If she focuses that untapped energy into her studies, she will be the most brilliant student in this college."

Puja received her education at Lakshmi Girls High School. She had a passion for dancing.

She had previously said, "Daddy, I want to continue dance classes in Miami. There is no emergency—only when you can afford to send me there, not at the present time."

The beauty about Puja is that she understood my financial limitations.

She always remarked, "When you can afford to buy what I need, Daddy, let me know, please."

Time flew by swiftly as I waited patiently for my daughter's assessment. The principal emerged smiling from the examination room with Puja at his side.

He said, "I am amazed that your daughter's grades are extremely high in this assessment. She will be placed in a class where children are two years older than her age. Here are all the documents for preparation to attend school in the morning. Sir, you have a brilliant child."

"Thank you, sir, for your time and patience. Puja will be in school in the morning. Have a nice day" was my humble reply.

I told Puja, "I am proud of you. My father had said to me, 'You have to reach for the skies'. My dear, I know you will reach for the skies. You will touch the skies. I know you will make me proud. Today's result in school is an indication that you have the potential to be the best in this school. Anyway, let us go to any restaurant of your choice—of course, within walking distance, since we do not have a vehicle."

Puja said, "Daddy, I will study to be the best. I do not like to be a follower. My determination is to be a leader. I strive to be the best in everything. Anyway, I love Wendy's. Daddy, let us go to Wendy's."

The restaurant was about half a mile from our apartment. We sat and ate a hearty meal.

Puja spoke nonstop on everything that concerned her.

I looked at my daughter's face and realized that I was not spending enough time with them. My limited time was busy organizing our survival here. I was neglecting my fatherly obligations in a big way. It was getting dark as we walked back to our apartment. As we approached our apartment, we noticed that there was blood stains on the door.

We rushed inside and noticed that Sandra, my wife, was lying on the inflatable mattress, with blood dripping profusely from her hand. Her countenance had changed to a dark pale color. She had fainted.

I shouted to Puja, "Rush to the lobby and call 911! Give them our address! Go now! Hurry up."

Hema was returning with Mala from the park. She started to cry when she saw the bloodstains.

I tried desperately to stop the bleeding. My wife was not fully cognizant of her surroundings. The neighbors had seen blood on the front door of the apartment, and they called the rescue. Fire rescue reached within ten minutes, and they were administering CPR to my wife.

The attendant said, "Sir, do you have insurance? We have to take your wife to the hospital. She must get stitches at once. Treatment at the hospital will be very expensive."

I answered quickly, "No, we do not have insurance, but I will pay for the services. We will go in the ambulance with her. Hema, come with me. Puja, stay and take care of Mala."

We were rushed to the hospital in the ambulance with the siren blaring. We reached the hospital in a few minutes. In the Emergency Room, we were greeted by a male nurse who examined the gaping wound. He asked, "Was this incident caused by a domestic dispute? Who was fighting, and who else is injured?"

"No," I said blatantly, "no one was fighting. We came to the apartment and found my wife bleeding on the floor."

He mockingly said, "Yeah, right."

He left with my wife to attend to her wounds.

During our stay at the hospital, we were visited by two officers. Their line of questioning made me feel like I was guilty of a crime. The officer was serious and said, "Look at the wound on her hand. That is where you stabbed her. This is a serious offence. Do you want a lawyer? Anything you say will be used against you at this moment. You people from the Middle East like to beat up women. You should be ashamed to assault a woman. In this country, this is a serious offence."

He pointed his finger near my face very menacingly.

Was this officer serious? He gave me the impression that jail was imminent for me.

For half an hour, the officer was questioning me. He was trying to intimidate me. From American movies, I knew that if one spoke rudely or shouted at the officers, then one would be arrested at once. I asked myself, was the officer trying to aggravate me to arrest me? I smiled as he spoke to me. I did not show any sign of anger or fear. They were not satisfied with my answers. Then they called my daughter Hema into a private room to question her separately. Hema spent about half an hour with the officers in a private room.

She returned with tears in her eyes. I hugged her, and she continued crying. Hema was not at home at the time of the incident. She was walking with Mala in the park. She returned when the fire rescue arrived at the apartment.

The officer said, "We will visit you at your apartment for further investigation into this matter in a few days. I need to speak to your wife before we leave here."

They visited my wife in the privacy of the hospital examination room.

I assumed the subject was domestic violence. There were serious consequences for these charges.

Hema said, "I told the officer that my daddy would not hurt a fly."

She told me that the officer said, "That is fine, he may not hurt a fly, but can he hurt your mother?"

Sandra was discharged from the hospital after five hours of treatment. She was weak but looked revived and alert. The nurse in the reception area said, "Your hospital expenses will be mailed to you in one month. Thank you for choosing our hospital."

We took a taxi and headed back to our apartment. Everyone was quiet in the taxi.

We were trying to digest the events that had transpired.

Sandra was unusually quiet in the taxi. I asked her, Are you okay?. What happened in the apartment?. How was there blood on the door?"

She said, "The drinking glass shattered on the tiles. When I went to clean the spill, I fell on the broken splinters. Then I fainted on the floor. I crawled to the door to get help but fainted".

"Understand something clearly—if we have any criminal record or any problem with the law, it will affect our chances of getting permanent residence or becoming citizens in this beloved America. Domestic violence is a serious problem. It is not only a problem but should be tolerated in any home." was my response.

The taxi driver was curious and listening attentively. He looked confused but did not join in the conversation. There was deadly silence for the rest of the journey.

The officer came the next day to continue their investigations on the incident.

They spoke to Puja who had just returned from her first day at school.

Puja told them, "My daddy and I saw Mommy bleeding when we returned from my school."

I think the investigating officers believed that there was a cover-up by the children.

Someone was hiding the truth. The two officers left the apartment with a closing remark that they will continue to monitor my family from time to time.

From this incident, I realized that it was easy to get someone in trouble with the law.

My finances were being depleted by unnecessary or unforeseen circumstances. The good news, though, was that our Florida identification cards arrived in the mail. Sadly, there were no funds to deposit in the bank. I spoke to my family about saving money and wasteful spending.

Those words fell on deaf ears. I wondered whether all immigrants undergo such extreme hardships.

CHAPTER SEVEN

A New Adventure

Two months after the hurricane devastated Naples, my friend Moe called on the telephone. He was crying. The sadness in his voice was heart breaking. He said, "This is the biggest nightmare that I have ever experienced in my lifetime. I witnessed Mother Nature at her most deadly moments. I saw large trees tossed in the wind like paper toys. The furious winds lifted trailer homes and parked them in lakes. Our windows into the hotel were smashed to shreds. Our vehicles were damaged beyond repair. This was a scene from a horror story. I do not know what to do at this time. It makes me wonder whether to restart the hotel. How can I cope with this tragedy of epic proportion? My family has nothing. The insurance company is not helping our situation."

My words to him were meant to provide comfort. "Hey, my friend, I know you are a fighter. You are going to bounce back, and business will be better. You are one of my heroes. I do not want to hear such discouraging talk from you. You have given me courage in the past. Now I am telling you to have courage and not give up.

"Everything will be all right. When I came here with nothing, you showed me the art of survival. In a way, you are very lucky. What about those people that have lost their family and property? You are still very fortunate. Come on, you have to keep on fighting."

Moe was extremely depressed. He was sobbing on the phone.

He continued, "My life's dreams shattered as we watched from the safety of our battered home. My family has nothing that encourages me to move forward."

I interrupted Moe from his negative and discouraging way of thinking.

My voice gained strength to encourage my depressed friend. "When I came to Florida, you showed me the way to succeed. You showed me how to survive and adapt to living in America. You told me that you captured the American dream. My family speaks very highly of your dreams, strength, and determination. This is America, where all dreams are possible. You are going to get bigger and better. Keep on fighting. I do not want to hear anymore discouraging talks. Go back and rebuild everything. Come on, keep on fighting.

"You are my American hero. Your family is depending on you for strength. You are a kind-hearted person. When everything fails, look to the skies and ask God to help."

Moe was been energized by my encouraging words.

His voice changed to the Moe that I first met. "My friend, you are so right. You speak from your heart. I needed that boost of confidence to move forward. Thank you. Now I am awake, and life goes on. Thank you, my friend.

"Oh yes, I want you to make one promise to me. After you pass the Pharmacy Board exam, please bring your family for a visit in Naples. That means you will have to drive your car to Naples."

Tears filled my eyes, and I said, "You will get your wish soon. Presently, we do not have a vehicle. Say a special hello to your family. Good-bye, my friend, and be strong. We missed your loving family. Give them my love. Good-bye, my friend, I will see you soon."

In my heart, there was a feeling that Moe would rebuild and grow stronger every day. My problems were minute compared to the disaster that changed the lives of millions of people in Naples. Your life can change in the blink of an eye. Therefore, we must enjoy life to the fullest and every

The American Dream

moment. After listening to Moe's tragedy, I decided to look at everything in a very positive way.

I started to look at all the positive aspects of my life. For example, with Moe's help, I was now working in a family oriented pharmacy. Their culture might have been different, but love and affection radiated from their hearts. In a short time, I was accepted as one of their most dedicated workers.

However, I stopped accepting coffee, much to the annoyance of my coworkers. My pharmacy manager treated me like a caring mother under her protected wings. My employer, Jose, treated me like a brother, with respect and dignity. A bicycle was now my means of transport to Sunset Pharmacy. Our lives were slowing evolving in a better way. A stronger foundation for my family lives was been established.

My two eldest daughters, Hema and Puja, had begged me to take them to Miami Seaquarium.

This was an opportunity to bond with them. This trip would be both educational and entertaining.

In a jovial conversation with my wife, we discussed the trip to the Seaquarium.

She remarked, "This is a waste of money. We can use the money for shopping. We do not have a vehicle. How are you going to get to the Seaquarium?" Any negative statement was not going to discourage me from planning or thinking about such a trip.

After the disaster in Naples, I decided that the time spent with the family was just as important as saving money. After all, my mother said that her children were her wealth.

How was this adventure to become a reality?

The journey was about twenty-five miles from our apartment to Miami Seaquarium. My two eldest daughters were ecstatic when the trip was discussed with them.

I had one week to plan as to what form of transportation would be most economical.

Riding my bicycle to work was less tiring than walking. On my way to Sunset Pharmacy, I spotted a fleet of taxis near our neighborhood supermarket.

This was a good opportunity to enquire about the cost of transportation for my planned trip. There were about ten taxis parked together. However, one taxi was parked separately from the others. I was embarrassed to be asking prices. This driver was standing by himself, listening to music. *Maybe he has no friends* was my impression.

The music was distinctly from Bollywood. This was the first time in Miami that I heard Hindi music.

"Namaste" was my greeting. My first impression was that he came from Punjab in India. In Trinidad; my pharmacy intern was a Sikh. He wore a turban every day. He cooked a lot of Punjabi foods for my staff in the pharmacy.He was a strong,kind and gentle person.He always had a radiant smile.

The taxi driver was wearing a distinct scarlet red turban that is associated with Sikhs from the state of Punjab. He clasped his two hands in a prayerlike fashion and replied, "Namaste, Bhai. Aap kaise hain?" (Meaning, "I greet you in the name of God, my brother. With respect, how are you?") He then said, "Bhai, what part of India are you from?"

I replied, "No, my forefathers came from India, but I grew up in Trinidad in the West Indies. My friend, my name is Moonan, and my family wants to go to the Seaquarium. What is the taxi fare for a round trip to Miami Seaquarium?"

With a distinct Punjabi accent, he smiled and said, "Mera naam Singh hai." (Meaning, "My name is Singh.") "I am going to give you a special price. I am going to charge one hundred and twenty-five dollars for your round trip.

That is the best price that you can get here. Check those drivers, they will tell you two hundred dollars."

This was definitely good news to my ears, so I said, "Okay, it is a deal. Here is my address. My family will be happy. Okay, sir, what time are we leaving on Sunday?"

With a distinct Indian accent, he said, "We will leave at eight o'clock in the morning to avoid the traffic. Then you can leave the Seaquarium at five o'clock."

I shook his hand to seal the deal.

Friday, at the pharmacy, everything went smoothly. Everyone wanted to finish his or her work on time to enjoy the weekend.

Dr. Maria called me in her office to speak to me. "My friend," she said very passionately, "remember, your Pharmacy Board examination is in one month. I do not want you to repeat this examination. I trust that you are burning the midnight's oil with your studies. You have to be very focused. The final goal is passing this exam. This is the most important exam in your life. Do not be an eternal pharmacy intern."

I thanked her for her concern. She was right. My studies had taken a back seat in my line of priorities.

At this time, I rushed to the bank to deposit my paycheck.

My favorite teller was waiting to serve me. She was pleasantly surprised that I had received my identification card.

I cycled home with the feeling of an inner peace.

My dad had told me, "True peace comes from within. When you are at peace with yourself, then you can radiate peace to others. Peace does not come from the barrel of a gun."

Mahatma Gandhi was quoted saying, "Each one has to find his peace from within, and peace to be real must be unaffected by outside circumstances."

Sunday morning was a big day for my family. That day, our long-awaited adventure to Miami Seaquarium was becoming a reality.

Apart from our trip to Naples, my family had never ventured any further than the shopping plaza in our neighborhood.

Early Sunday morning, Hema and I prepared our favorite Trinidadian dish called *pelau*.

It is a one-pot dish made from chicken, rice, tomatoes, beans, carrots, and coconut milk.

It is very delicious and tasty. My plan was to have a meal before we entered the Seaquarium compound. Everyone packed extra clothing for this trip.

My backpack was very heavy. My wife had packed food and clothing for a week.

We were ready to go on our journey.

Singh was waiting in the lobby of the apartment. He was very punctual. He greeted us, saying, "Namaste, how are you all?"

Hema and Puja responded "namaste" with clasped hands.

We hurriedly packed our belongings into the trunk of the taxi.

My family was introduced to Mr. Singh. My two eldest daughters were asking Singh a lot of questions as we proceeded on our journey. They were curious because in Trinidad, my pharmacist intern was a Sikh. His name was also Singh. Our taxi driver was delighted to answer any question. "I came to Miami when I was small like baby Mala. My father migrated from India during the war with Pakistan. I still practice our Sikhism culture. It is a religion popular in Punjab. I have two children that live here in Miami."

Hema was quick to ask Singh, "Mr. Singh, do you eat chicken? Because I made a dish called *pelau* that you can try when we reach to the Seaquarium."

Singh laughed and said, "You know, I feel at home with you all. It is not easy living here, wearing a turban. You look like Middle Eastern, especially after 9/11. People look at us with fear and suspicion. Passengers are afraid to come in my taxi. I know that is true, but what can you do? We have to enjoy life and not worry."

"My friend," I said, "can you give us an idea of famous places and historic sites along the route?"

With that suggestion, Singh started talking nonstop about the route and places along the way. We felt like tourists in a foreign land. We reached Key Biscayne, and Singh stopped the vehicle. He motioned us to exit the vehicle.

His face broke into a smile, and he said, "This is my favorite area. From this bridge, you can see the Miami bayfront."

"Wow! Look at the magnificent view! This is unmatched anywhere in the world!" The view was picturesque and breathtaking. Our designated photographer, Puja, was busy taking numerous photos. After half an hour, we continued our journey.

From the bridge, we saw white sandy beaches.

Our journey lasted about one hour. We enjoyed the drive to the Seaquarium. Everyone was talking and laughing, including our driver.

He made our trip educational and relaxing. Now, we sat to eat our famous *pelau*.

I turned to Singh and said, "Thank you for the educational tour of Miami. I know my family learnt a lot from you today. We cannot afford a vehicle at this time. Therefore, I welcome your knowledge of Miami to my family. My friend, before you depart from here, can you try some of our famous *pelau*?"

Singh smiled broadly and said, "Thank you. I am hungry. I am glad that you asked me because the smell of the food made me very hungry. *Pelau* sounds delicious."

Our kind-hearted taxi driver shared our meal. He said the food was extremely delicious.

He added, "Can I have some to take away?"

Hema rushed to fulfill his request.

He departed with the promise to return at five in the afternoon.

Mother Nature cooperated and gave us a cool, calm day. The white puffy clouds sheltered us from the overhead sun. There was a gentle sea breeze stroking our faces. The Miami Seaquarium was ideally located near the seaside. My family was very excited. We were taking photos of everything. We followed the map as a guide. Our first stop was "The killer Whale."

There were many people waiting for this performance. Hema, Puja, and I sat in the front row. We were warned that the whale would splash icy water on us. That was not a problem. We were there to have a good time.

Sandra and Mala sought refuge on the higher seats to prevent the cold water from splashing on them. There was some calypso and steel band music to start the show.

People were dancing, and Hema and Puja joined in the festivities. Trinidad is the land and home of steel band and calypso.

The show was about to begin. The killer whale made its appearance.

The performance was magnificent. The massive whale splashed cold, icy water in the front seats about three consecutive times. We were freezing but were also having fun. The show was fantastic. I wondered why a giant whale was living in such a small-enclosed area. Was this mammal happy? Whales enjoy swimming in large open areas. In their natural habitat, they can swim a hundred miles in a day.

Our next stop was a visit to the dolphins. We were overwhelmed by their grace and beauty. They were performing acrobatics, jumping high above the waters.

The astounding performances of the dolphins were well received by the zestful crowd. Then we visited the place where they were feeding the sharks. We saw the razor-like teeth of the sharks.

They could devour anything with those saw-like teeth. We moved along to the menacing crocodiles.

My wife said, "Those are big like the one that got killed in the Everglades. They can easily swallow a human being."

We saw a variety of multicolored birds—from toucans, parrots, and cockatiels to flamingoes. I remembered my singing friend from our apartment. He had disappeared after the hurricane. I missed my feathered friend; maybe one day he would return to entertain us. My family was hungry again. We went to the restaurant and ordered burgers and fries. The place was spacious and clean. We sat and relaxed in the air conditioned room. Everyone was having a good time in this family oriented park. Everyone in my family was enjoying themselves.

We rested for a short while and continued our sightseeing and shows. The sea-lion show was amusing and entertaining. This is what my family wanted a time to relax away from the confines of the apartment.

We took many fun photos throughout the day. The weather had changed by three o'clock; it was sweltering hot and humid. There was a miniature version of a water park. I took charge of Mala, and the rest of my family went to enjoy the cool soothing water. I walked with Mala and showed her the waterfall that caused her to smile. The water vapors falling on her face provided a soothing effect. After half an hour, I motioned my family that it was time to move on. Our final stop was the giant aquatic mammal called the manatee.

They are herbivorous. They were feeding on cabbage and carrots and swimming lazily in their small-enclosed area. They were about twelve feet in length and weighed about one thousand pounds.

Our memorable day had unfortunately ended.

Time had flown by quickly.

Singh, our driver, was waiting patiently in the car park. Our hearts remained behind at the Seaquarium. Singh had brought two passengers in his taxi. They were his daughters. He greeted us, saying, "Namaste, Bhai. How was your day?"

Hema and Puja answered, "Funtastic!.Again We say Funtastic was our day"

Puja interrupted, "My goodness, it was great! I could not have asked for a better day!"

Singh continued, "These are my two princess. They were teenagers like Hema and Puja." My daughters were very pleased to meet them. They started to talk nonstop about anything and everything. Singh continued, "You all said that you wanted to bathe in the beach. Let us go. I am going to stop for one hour." My family could not have been happier by this change of events.

My daughters were talking to Singh's children as if they were old acquaintances. Everyone was enjoying the crystal-clear waters. The four teenagers were splashing and frolicking in the water. Singh and I were all alone. Suddenly, tears poured from his eyes, and he lamented, "My children are my happiness. They are my weakness and my strength.They are my life. However, I can only see them on weekends.

I am divorced about five years ago. This life is unfair.I can tell you again and again that this life is really unfair. My children love to spend time with me.

I love my kids like my life. I do not have any steady income. My income depends on the demands of the public for a taxis service. She is truly a *neemakaram*. My exwife as if she was my goddess. She was the angel of my life. I loved her with all my heart".

Those words were full of passion and radiated from the bottom of his heart.

Tears flooded my eyes for this innocent victim.

I reached and hugged him. I tried to console him with soothing words, but he just wanted someone to listen to his troubles. Sometimes, it is better that you listen and not offer advice.

He continued becoming very emotional. "There was nothing that my wife wanted that I did not give her. I made love to her as a man does to his wife. I sacrificed my happiness and comfort just to make her happy. I brought her flowers and gifts regularly. I took my family shopping to the mall anytime she requested. I was always there for my family at the expense of my work. Be careful, my friend, life is not easy. Your happiness can change in the blink of an eye. Someone can take away your happiness like a thief in the night."

Singh wiped the tears from his eyes and signaled his daughters that it was time to leave.

I took a deep breath and looked to the heavens. I guess, for that day, I had to enjoy the joyous precious moments, wait, and see what the next day would bring.

We departed into the sunset, away from a memorable experience. My family was very hungry again.

I told Singh, "My friend, there is a Chinese buffet on Eight street. I want to buy dinner for you and your family."

His daughters were delighted. It meant spending more time with their new friends.

Everyone enjoyed the buffet. We proceeded to our apartment. That day, my family had a variety of meals. For breakfast, they enjoyed a Trinidad dish. Then for lunch, they had American burgers. For dinner, we enjoyed a Chinese meal. That is total adaptation to the American cuisine. We reached our apartment by eight o'clock.

Our teenage girls exchanged addresses and phone numbers. They promised to keep in touch on the weekends. I gave Singh the money that he agreed for the journey. He returned twenty-five dollars to me.

I said, "My friend, no, please keep the twenty-five dollars. I appreciate the gesture, but you spent a lot of time and gasoline on this trip. Please keep in touch."

I placed the money back in his hands. I had found another great person in this taxi driver. Greatness is not measured in how much wealth you accumulate but by how much you are willing to help someone. That day, I was touched by the man from Punjab, my friend Mr. Singh.

After this day, my family never saw Singh again. Was his child-support payment very high that he could not meet his court's decree?

Was he in jail, or did he return to India? We never found the answer. My family wondered about the fate of a humble but most pleasant taxi driver.

CHAPTER EIGHT

Failure Strikes Hard from Within and Without

It was three weeks to my State Board examination. My mind was deep in thought as I rode my bicycle to work at Sunset Pharmacy. My memories flew back to Trinidad at our University of the West Indies. Everything was clear in my mind as though it was yesterday. Time has gone by, but fond memories of my time at this great institute of learning lingers vividly in my mind—memories of my dedicated lectures who instilled the spirit of professionalism into hearts and minds.

They taught us to be proud of our profession and always let our lives be a true reflection of being a pharmacist. They taught us to love our profession but also to be humble human beings. Such was the selfless dedication of my lecturers, working long and tedious hours beyond the call of duty—men like Dr. Narinesingh, Dr. Ramnarine, Mr. Guiness, and Mr. Rahaman, who worked with me and molded my life in the right direction.

I looked to the heavens, said "Thank you", and continued my ride to Sunset Pharmacy. With my upcoming examinations, I knew that I had to burn the midnight oil to pass this examination. The problem was balancing my bill payments and my pharmacy examinations. Working extra hours at the pharmacy was necessary to maintain a decent standard of living. My bills were coming fast and furious. On the other hand, it was necessary to spend a lot of time studying.

I reached the pharmacy and greeted everyone with my usual Hispanic salutations. It was a long, tiring day.

Dr. Maria said with a concerned look, "Moonan, we have to finish all the medications for the homes. Tonight and tomorrow night, be prepared to work until midnight. We have to work steadfast to ensure that we meet our target."

I needed the overtime salary, but my studies were being neglected. How do I balance in this dilemma?

The pharmacy team worked feverishly to meet our targets. There was an abundance of coffee. Everyone drank throughout the fifteen hours of work. We finished at midnight. We departed to our respective homes. I rode my bicycle carefully to my apartment.

The night was pitching black. It was about one o'clock when I reached my apartment.

My wife was awake and watching television in the living room. The children were snoring in the bedroom.

Sandra was visibly upset and asked me, "Are you sure you are coming from the pharmacy at this ungodly hour? In Trinidad, you never worked so late in your own pharmacy."

I replied, "My dear, you are not living in Trinidad. Jose said that we have to finish all the medications for all homes by tomorrow. We have no choice but to work late. Everyone had to work late. Listen, I am not the boss here. When they say jump, I ask them how high. I feel that I am carrying the world on my shoulders. I need your support, and I feel that it is not forthcoming. How can we survive if I do not work extra hours? We desperately need extra money."

She continued her argument. "Maybe you have a woman, and you are hanging out late. I feel that you are lying to me. Which pharmacy is opened at this ungodly hour?"

I was getting upset with this line of questioning.

I interjected, "Can you call the pharmacy tomorrow night? Dr. Maria said we have to work late again. Anyway, this is not the time for an argument."

My children were sound asleep. Therefore, argument at this ungodly hour was wisely out of the question.

The previous day, Puja had left a note from her teacher for my attention.

My wife should have taken care of the problem, but Puja insisted that her father take care of her issue.

My morning started very early in the pharmacy again. My body was extremely exhausted mentally and physically. My tired body had no time for a blissful rest.

Jose had decreed that his staff finish the homes regardless of the time. Again, we finished at midnight. This time, I was greeted outside the pharmacy with showers of blessing.

What choice did I have except to ride home as fast as possible? Within a few minutes of leaving the pharmacy, my clothes were soaking wet. The road was pitch dark. With the intermittent shower, riding was proving to be most difficult. Suddenly, something or someone hit my bicycle, and it somersaulted out of control. My right hand plowed into the solid ground.

The whole world was spinning around me. My right hand was bleeding profusely. The back tire of the bicycle was bent slightly. There was a throbbing pain radiating from my damaged hand.

I limped slowly home. On reaching my apartment, my family was asleep. My wounds needed medical attention. My body was dead tired. Within minutes, my inflatable bed was my refuge.

Puja woke up early in the morning for school. As she entered the living room, she shouted, "Daddy, you are bleeding! What happened?" She came and hugged me tightly.

"Honestly, I do not know. I felt something hit my bicycle, but it was pitch dark. I am okay. However, I have to return to the pharmacy in one hour," I replied, looking at my wounds.

My wife added sarcastically, "Are you sure you were not in a fight? You look like someone beat you up. I do not believe you are working in the pharmacy until midnight."

My mother had said, "Words do not kill. Harsh words do not kill. Learn to smile at harsh words. It does no harm to you. Learn to ignore it. Like the ill wind, it blows away." My parents had become immune to verbal abuse. After working for their British Colonial masters, insults were just ignored like a passing wind. To coexist, I was learning to adopt that concept, whether at home or at work.

I told Puja, "My dear, your mummy can go with you to school."

Puja gave me that pathetic look, saying, "No, Daddy, I want you to come to my school when you have the time."

Time was going by quickly. "Okay, I will talk to you when I return from work today. Guys, have a nice day."

My bicycle was still in working condition. My right hand was in pain from bruises on my fingers. At the pharmacy, everyone was concerned about my hand. I told them that I fell from the stairs.

Jose said jokingly, "Ah, my friend, your wife beat you up last night when you were sleeping."

I thought that was funny. The day passed uneventfully at the pharmacy.

That day, in my apartment, my studies were going to be a priority.

That evening, as I tried to focus on my studies, Puja came to me. She looked sad and very disturbed. I hugged her as she sat next to me. I said to her, "Where is that Puja smile that makes me want to hug you?"

Tears came to her eyes. She sobbed uncontrollably.

"Daddy, I do not want to go back to that school. All the children are mean and nasty to me. My complexion is different from theirs. Therefore, they make all kinds of jokes about me. They write abusive notes on my desk. They are bullies. I cannot focus on my studies. My grades are not going to be good. They are ignorant of my culture, but they make stupid comments."

I hugged her and said, "You cannot run every time you are bullied or someone does not like you. You cannot change your complexion, but you can show them you are more mature than them. Do me one favor, and listen to this. For one term, show them that you are brighter and more intelligent than they are.

Get honor grades and see what happens. I am going to make an appointment to speak to the principal about your concerns. My dear, do not get discouraged and upset your future. One day, the same students will ask for your help. You are a Baijoo. Show me your determination to prove that those ignorant children are dead wrong about you."

The rest of my family were listening. We spoke for half an hour about Puja's concerns.

Now, it was time to focus on my studies. Every night, for the next three weeks, I burnt the midnight's oil, engrossed in my studies.

My Pharmacy Board examinations consisted of two parts. Part One was a law examination. Part Two was more on medications, drug interactions, calculations, and clinical pharmacy.

Prepared or not, my exam day was here. The examination was held in the Blue Lagoon Centre.

My taxi reached there one hour before my examination. This gave me the opportunity to do some much-needed last minute revising. I took some deep breaths and put a positive attitude toward passing this that day. The tests were being administered under the watchful eyes of cameras.

I sat and patiently read and answered every question. Dr. Maria was right on target: the examination was difficult. Many questions centered on hospital pharmacy. I had no training or experience in that field. I tried my best to answer every question under those circumstances.

Three weeks later, my results arrived by mail at Sunset Pharmacy. My hand trembled as I read the results.

In both examinations, I failed by a small percentage of points. Suddenly, my future in Florida looked grim. Tears filled my eyes. My confidence as a person ebbed slowly away.

Dr. Maria came to me with words of consolation. "Moonan, do not worry. Next time, you are going to pass with flying colors. Focus on getting better results. Go home and take a rest."

Dr. Maria was right on target. There was too much distraction with my life.

The bearer of bad news had reached our apartment. My family was sad but understanding about my results.

Hema and Puja tried to cheer me up. I was very depressed and disappointed. I walked to the porch. Hema and Puja came and sat quietly by my side.

I pondered and bowed my head, then spoke, "You know, we cannot survive here with my pharmacy intern salary. Today, I am fearful our future is uncertain and bleak."

Hema interrupted, saying, "Today, I read a statement from your guru, Sai Baba, about fear. Fear is nothing but a bundle of negative thoughts. Counter it with positive thoughts. Daddy, failure is part of life. You taught me that last year. Just keep on studying and you will pass your examinations next time with flying colors."

Puja added, "Yes, Daddy, you said 'Never give up, and fight to make your dreams a reality.' When bullying was a problem, you taught me how to deal with it. I am not fearful again because of what you told me."

My wife and baby Mala joined the discussions. Looking at the darkness of the night, for the first time, I was unable to see a light at the end of the tunnel.

However, my ambition to become a Licensed Pharmacist in the United States of America superseded my fear, depression, and failures. My struggle to succeed seemed to be more intense and required more sacrifice.

Abraham Lincoln said, "My great concern is not whether you have failed but whether you are content with your failure."

Failure is a word that I do not tolerate. Tomorrow will be another day to fight for my future. With open arms, it is going to be a good fight—a fight to succeed for a better future.

CHAPTER NINE

The Strategy for Success: Home Run

Failure is not an option. Failure is not a word in my vocabulary. To my children, that word does not exist in their vocabulary.

Failure will come, but determination supersedes failures.

That day was the dawn of a new beginning. My determination to succeed in my pharmacy examination was paramount.

The question was who was going to help me with my studies? Hema volunteered to help me unconditionally. She was going to assist me to organize my course of studies and act as my secretary but without any salary.

She was to make sure that I adhered to my study schedules, and she helped me obtain additional information on my projects. Every night, she would revise with me a question-and-answer project. Every Saturday and Sunday, I would be spending alone in the library in the neighborhood or at home without unnecessary disturbances.

Dr. Maria and Jose were informed that for the next three months, there would be no overtime for me at the pharmacy.

Jose was very upset about my decision. On the other hand, Dr. Maria was in full support of my contingency plans. "My friend," Jose said sarcastically, "what about my medications for all the homes? Moonan, you are the centre of this work now. Please, at least work until six o'clock every day. When we are finished with the homes, then you can leave."

Dr. Maria interrupted, saying, "Jose, your work is very important, but Moonan needs his time to study. I do not want him failing again. He is only asking to work forty hours a week. Do not worry; you will get your homes completed on schedule. Give Moonan his time to study. He needs to focus on his studies. You will benefit the most when he passes the Board examinations."

Jose was not pleased with this conversation with Dr. Maria. He rushed out of the pharmacy, visibly upset.

She continued in my presence, "Moonan, take all the time that you need to study. You have to focus on your future. You did not come to United States to be an everlasting pharmacist intern. When it is the time to leave the pharmacy, just clock your card and leave. Go home, and focus on your studies. Do not waste time. Every moment is precious for your success. I repeat, do not waste precious time. You will live to regret it."

I thanked Maria for her support and cooperation.

She laughed loudly and said, "We have to stand up for each other as professionals. Jose wants the medications for homes finished to get more money. I want to ensure that you pass your State Board examination. That is why I'm your preceptor. I am your teacher. Do not let Jose bother you. I will deal with him."

For the next three months, studying was my priority.

Hema jokingly said, "Daddy, I am going to train you for a championship fight. You are under my training. There is focus and concentration. There is an allocated sleeping time. There is no gain without pain. We are going to make a rigid schedule for your studies."

Every night, Hema would spend time with me until two in the morning. My sleeping time was allocated to four hours per night. She quizzed me with multiple-choice questions. She was determined that I succeed at any cost. She pushed my mental and physical levels to the maximum limit of my endurance.

Her help and presence was a boost to my confidence. We covered all aspects of pharmacy from calculations, law, community, hospital, and mail order.

My weekends were spent in the library or studying quietly. The librarian was extremely helpful in her desire to see me succeed in my examination.

She said, "I admire people coming from foreign countries. They come and utilize all our facilities here. Children that are citizens here do not understand how fortunate they are to have these facilities.

They do not understand that libraries are like lighthouses erected in the sea of time. Knowledge comes from utilizing our unlimited resources. I love to see people of all ages utilizing our facilities."

"Thank for all the help. I am very fortunate to have met you. Your sincere desire for me to succeed is humbly appreciated" was my earnest reply.

My big examination day finally appeared. My confidence oozed through my body. My fear and idea of failing was replaced by positive vibrations. I wrote both examinations with more courage and conviction to succeed than my previous time.

Two weeks later, the Pharmacy Board sent a letter to my apartment. The results were overwhelming. Moonan had passed with flying colors. With bended knees and tears in my eyes, I thanked God for having given me the pleasure of serving the people of United States.

There was no phone card in my possession, so I hurried to the nearby gas station to purchase one. My friend, Samir, from Pakistan was not there. I wondered what had happened to him.

I called from the telephone in the apartment lobby to Trinidad. Jewan, my son, came on the telephone. I said zestfully, "Son, I am now qualified as a pharmacist in Florida. I passed my examinations with flying colors."

Jewan was extremely happy to hear the good news. "That is fantastic, Dad! I am so happy for you. This is the best news ever. My studies at the university is going very well. Daddy, I am proud of you." He was ecstatic in his response.

We spoke for about ten minutes. My parents were excited to speak to me.

My mother added, "Sita Ram, beta." (Meaning, in Hindi, "Greetings in the name of God, my son.") "Jewan told us the wonderful news. We are happy for you. Do not forget us here. Please come and visit us soon. We are dying to hug you again."

She started to cry, but it was tears of either happiness or loneliness, tears that her son was improving the quality of his life in America. Our conversations continued with my ten brothers and sisters.

This was the moment that everyone was waiting—that I was now a registered pharmacist in America. Eventually, the phone card was utilized, and the conversations finished abruptly.

Jose had stopped by my apartment to discuss my working schedule for the pharmacy. He was visibly upset that I had been working reduced hours for the last three months.

Now the table was turned in my favor, I decided to poke a little fun at Jose's immature behavior.

"My friend," Jose said sadly, "you have to work later hours to ensure the pharmacy runs smoothly. Please, I need you to work more hours to finish the homes. I need your practical knowledge in my pharmacy throughout the day."

"No, sir, I cannot work anymore hours as an intern for you. I quit working as an pharmacist intern for you, effective immediately," I replied with a sad and pathetic look.

"What do you mean that you quit? Please, Moonan, do not quit working. I need you desperately in my pharmacy. You are an integral part of my staff. I beg you not to quit your job," Jose said, pleading to me. His face turned red from my conversation.

"However, my intern days are behind me. Now I can work as a registered pharmacist in your pharmacy. I have the results and certification as a pharmacist. I was just messing with your mind," I answered, laughing heartily.

Jose hugged me as if he had found a long-lost friend and said, "Let us go and celebrate. Where do you want to go? Casinos, clubs, gambling or anyway you want. I will pay for whatever you want. Now you are more important to me, my friend."

Jose was extremely happy with the good news.

"Maybe another day. However, my family wants to prepare a special lunch for all your staff. I need your help in transporting everything to the pharmacy. Now I can work any hours that you will request in the future" was my reply to Jose.

My family had entered the apartment as we were speaking.

Jose shouted, "Moonan passed his pharmacy examinations!"

The American Dream

I showed everyone my results. There were tears of joy flowing abundantly.

Hema received a special hug for working assiduously with me.

Jose departed in a jovial manner. He promised to provide all the assistance in transporting the meals for my beloved coworkers.

We organized a scrumptious lunch for all the staff at Sunset Pharmacy. It was a combination of Caribbean and East Indian food. Then my last gift was a floral arrangement for Dr. Maria.

I wrote on the card, "Words cannot tell the appreciation and motherly love you have shown me. Your selfless acts of kindness and professional wisdom are the cornerstone to my success. You taught me. You nurtured me like your family. You molded me in Florida with your gentle but firm hands. I am eternally grateful. Thank you kindly and fellow pharmacist, Moonan."

Everyone enjoyed the variety of dishes that my family had prepared. Dr. Maria and her staff were elated. As the flowers were given, tears poured from Dr. Maria's eyes. She showed me the passionate side of her character. Jose's wife was there too, enjoying the food.

She came to me, laughing, and said, "Remember, I told you that you will pass with flying colors. Congratulations. Jose and I are proud of your success."

Another grueling day in the pharmacy had finally ended.

Everything in nature seemed to smile at me as I cycled back home. Now there was hope for a better and brighter tomorrow.

The sun was sinking in the western horizon.

The sun's rays tried to burst through the darkened clouds There was a ray of hope that life was going to improve or like the Jefferson's, "We are moving on up."

Confucius said, "Our greatest glory is not in ever falling, but in rising every time we fall."

CHAPTER TEN

Deception and Divorce

Time has flown very swiftly by. It was one and a half years since my family arrived in the beautiful sunny Florida. My bicycle was not my mode of transport to Sunset Pharmacy anymore. Now, I have purchased a used Toyota SUV. It is very old but a reliable form of transport. At least, the rains do not hinder my reaching to work drenched to the bones.Cycling kept me in strong physical shape.Now,I wondered whether I would gain a lot of weight.

Jose, at Sunset Pharmacy said,

"Riding a bicycle to the pharmacy did not reflect my professional status.

Your image should reflect your profession. Image is everything. You must portray a certain image as a professional"

That concept was of no consequence to me. Whether I walked, rode my bicycle or drove an old SUV, I am the same person.

The pleasant memories are still fresh in my mind about cycling to work. In many ways, I missed the joys of riding and getting drenched with the rain. Life is like riding a bicycle around a corner or in the darkness of the night. You cannot foresee what fortune or dangers lurk around the bend.

Hema was now back in college, pursuing a degree program at Florida International College in Computer studies. Puja was still in Middle school. She was an honor student.

She overcame bullying and loved attending school. She was regular and punctual in school. Mala was now in Daycare. Mala was not baby Mala anymore. She was now walking and was a little chatterbox. She was talkative like her elder sisters.

There is an inner satisfaction knowing that your hard work has laid a solid foundation for your family. There is a sense of relief that everything is finally going smoothly in your life. There is a sense of satisfaction in knowing that you have conquered your biggest demons and obstacles through hard work and sacrifice.

I had laid the solid foundation and was satisfied that my life would be easier in the near future. My wife, Sandra was now employed at a nearby Dollar Store. Working at the Dollar Store had transformed her to a more outspoken person. She called it woman power and equality. My opinion is better that you can be humble and strong at the same time.

She told me bluntly,

"Now I am working for my own money. Therefore, I want my own bank account. I want to spend my own money. With my salary, I want no one to interfere with my money."

I was smiling but was also totally baffled,

"But we have a joint bank account together. What is the problem? Nobody tells you anything about your spending".

She continued,

"I do not want to be accountable to anyone. I just want to manage my own money."

"That is fine. I have no problem with separate account," I said, laughing heartily.

When Sandra enters the apartment, there would be a distinct nauseating smell of cigarettes. Upon being asked, she said, "My coworkers are all smokers. Therefore, my clothes smell of cigarette. That is the simple true."

"My dear, understand that cigarette smoking is dangerous to your children's health" was my advice to her.

"We are in America. If I want to smoke then that should be my right" was her rude answer.

"True, you are so right but protect the health of your children in this tiny apartment. Secondary smoke is more dangerous than a smoker. Please think about your children's health first and foremost'. was my firm answer.

Sandra hardly spends time with the family. This strange behavior seemed that maybe someone had entered her life.

One night as the children were asleep, I decided to confront Sandra with my suspicion. I sat on the patio patiently awaiting her return from work. There was a strange loneliness that crept inside my body. A feeling that was alien and extremely uncomfortable. Was this feeling a premonition of bad events to follow in my life? This strange feeling engulfed my body like a shroud of unwelcome negative emotions My body shivered with mixed emotions.

As Sandra opened the apartment door, I reached to greet her. She turned her face away from me and disregarded my salutations. Lowering my voice so that our children will not be awakened, I motioned my wife to come and sit on the patio.

In a very low voice, I said

"We must have a serious talk at this time. You are treating me like a total stranger. You hardly spend time at home. Please tell me the truth of what is really happening in your life?

Sandra was furious and interrupted me with a loud voice,

I want a new and different life. I want to do what is best for my life. My feelings for you have died awhile ago. I do not love you anymore. My divorce papers are already filed and they will be served by police officers soon to you.

I felt like a ghost. Not a word came from my mouth. I was struck speechless.

Sandra was not remorseful or sorry for her actions. Not a drop of tear came from her eyes. She hurried to our bedroom and slammed the door shut. Tonight my inflatable bed in the living room will be my friend and comfort.

Hundreds of thoughts ran through my mind. You wonder whether it is your fault that this has happened, and what could have been done to prevent it. Sometimes, people just believe that they can vastly improve their lives if they find someone else. Ambition to improve ourselves is imbedded in our nature even at the expense of others, whether it is justified or not.

The world that we came to build in America was about to crumble to dust.

With that statement, Sandra walked out of my life. This was exactly what my taxi driver friend, Singh, had predicted happens when people file for a divorce.

All the elements were falling in place. Hiring a lawyer was out of the question; my joint account was depleted.

My coworkers watched with concern that another marriage had gone down the drain. Some of them had similar experiences of this ordeal in their lives. According to my fellow worker you hope for the best in a bad situation.

My protector and Hispanic mother, Dr. Maria was fuming mad,

"You came here to build a future and to make your family happy. That is something that I do not tolerate lightly. While you were climbing the ladder of success, tragedy strikes like a thief in the night. I have seen you come here and work with wet clothes from the rain. You spent every cent to make your family happy. Where have all the good and honest people gone?

You sacrificed everything to make your family happy. Life is a strange experience. Sometimes the good one suffers. Moonan, I am very sorry. We will support you and be here for you. Where have all the faithful people in the world gone?"

Dr. Maria wept bitterly as if someone had hurt her own flesh and blood.

All my fellow workers were sympathetic toward my dilemma. Some of them had come from Cuba and faced a similar problem here. Cultures and languages may be different, but the understanding, love, and compassion are the same thing. This was my extended American family. They sympathized with me as if I was their flesh and blood.

I did not know the system of divorce. Therefore, I signed all the necessary documents that her lawyers had sent to me. Memories of the taxi driver, Singh, lingered in my mind. Now I understood the frustration and helplessness that Singh had undergone. Your hands are tied in despair, and you sit and see where the lots are cast. You see everything that you build crumble around you. There is nothing that can be done to stop the decay.

We got divorced on the first court hearing. The court allowed me visitations rights on weekend visitations to see Mala.

I explained to Hema and Puja that I had to work extra hours for six months to pay the court order or I would have to go to jail. My daughters understood and helped each other throughout the time that I was working. I volunteered to work any and every overtime that was available, my income at Sunset Pharmacy could not absorb all the new bills entrusted on me. Therefore, my intention was to get another source of income. To forget all my financial woes, I decided to visit my friend Moe in Naples.

When I called Moe, he was ecstatic.

"Are you driving a car to come to Naples or riding your bicycle to my home?. After all, it is only about a three hours drive with a car and maybe walking will get you here in two days. When are you coming? Please spend a full week with us or maybe two weeks. I have so much to discuss with you. My family talks about you every day. Remember the best fishing is still here in Naples. My family will be glad to hear the good news"

"My friend," I said, "I am sorry, my friend, but the children are in school. Another time we will see, if that is possible. We will just come for the weekend. There is so much we have to talk about. So many things have changed so drastically. We must sit and have a serious talk. I need your advice"

Moe added, "How is Sandra?"

I hesitated for a minute, then added,

"Oh, she is all right. Hey, my friend, we will come Friday night and leave Sunday afternoon. Is that okay with you?"

"Great, see you Friday night."

With those words, I said goodnight to Moe. No mention was made about my divorce to him.

There is a psychological dilemma that every divorce person undergoes a few weeks after separation. They blame themselves for the breakup because of a lot of reasons. They think that enough time was not spent with the estranged partner or enough love was not given.

However, sometimes, roving eyes find new excitement in an outside relationship.

That evening, I called Trinidad and spoke to my family about the events that transpired. They were devastated about the divorce. They told me that life is unpredictable and to put my best foot forward. However, my son had very good news that he was moving to final year at the university. Like my other children, he was an honor student. I was very proud of his achievements.

My dad was sad as he came to speak to me on the phone. "Forget the past, and move on with your life. I raised you to be strong and courageous. You will overcome all obstacles in your pathway. Listen, forget the past and move on. No good is going to come about discussing divorce. Pick up the pieces and move forward with improving your life."

"But, Dad, life is not fair," I interjected.

My dad was visibly upset. "No, but-but, Son, I say again, pick up the pieces and move on. Yes, life is never fair, but you are strong and healthy. In everything, look at the positive side of life. Talk to God as though he is your friend. He will help you always. You have problems, then find solutions. No one is going to spoon-feed you. All my life, I have been a fighter. You are the same way. You will overcome all obstacles and grow stronger. The more you dwell on the past, the more you will feel extremely hurt. One day, you will find an honest and a beautiful woman to love you. Meanwhile, focus on rebuilding your life. Another thing that is very important, do not let your children suffer because you are divorced. Now is the time that they need a strong father."

"Thank you, Dad. I needed to hear those comforting and reassuring words."

He was silent after that conversation on the telephone.

My trip to Naples was uneventful. My three daughters were quiet and sad. I realized that I must encourage my daughters to be happy.

"In the morning, all of us are going fishing with Moe," I said.

Hema jumped in. "Fishing? Are you serious? Yes, of course. I love to fish. Besides, it is relaxing in Naples."

Puja added, "Daddy, last time we were here in Naples, you did not take me fishing."

This was the right note to give them words of encouragement. "I am sorry. When I am not working on the weekend, I will take you all fishing in the Everglades. Listen, girls, we have each other, and we have to learn how to survive without your mother. I promise that I am going to be there for you all. We have to work as a team. Talk to me as though I am both your father and mother. Whatever problems you encounter, I will stand with you, whatever the circumstances. You are not alone" was my reassurance to my three angels.

Then I heard that familiar friendly chatter from my daughters. I wondered whether they felt that I would abandon them at their most vulnerable time.

We reached Naples at ten that night. We were greeted by Moe's family. Moe and Sita hugged me as if I was a long-lost brother. They were extremely happy that we had come to spend the weekend with them. Naples felt like my first home in Florida.

I felt like a refugee in a safe haven. All my feelings of despair and hopelessness had disappeared. Was it the tranquil environment or the perfect aura that this family exuded?

Moe's wife said, "Where is Sandra? I believe that something is drastically wrong. What is going on here?"

I replied, looking at Sita, "That is a long story."

They ushered us quickly inside their hotel. It was November, and the temperature was colder than the previous months. They had prepared a scrumptious dinner just for my family. Moe's children were busy talking to my children about everything. They were glad for the company, especially children of the same age. After dinner, all the children retreated to the living room to play video games.

Moe and Sita listened attentively to what had transpired. They were understanding and sympathetic to my problem.

Moe's advice to me was, "Avoid your ex-wife. All conversations between both of you have to be about the

THE AMERICAN DREAM

children. Do not meet in a lonely place with her. If possible, have another person present, or the children, when you are having a conversation with your ex-wife.

"The only way out of your financial crisis is to find a night job. Do not work on weekends. You will see great rewards by spending time with your children.

"Apply to Hurts Rx drugstore for employment. They need a nighttime pharmacist. You can work two nights weekly. That should pay for your court order. Now, your children should be your priority. They need you now more than ever. They did not ask for this to happen, so support them in every way. You are their tower of strength. Whatever you do from now on, they will copy your example.

"It takes two parties to make a marriage work. When one is not happy, the marriage is eventually broken. Then they become like bitter enemies. Love is replaced by hatred. Divorce means a separation. All the bridges of love have been burnt to the ground. So move on."

I answered confidently, "My friend and brother, I will follow your advice. My children will not suffer in any way. Anyway, we want to go fishing in the morning."

When Hema and Puja heard the word "fishing," they rushed into the room to ensure they were included in our fishing expedition. The children played all night in the living room. I slept comfortably on the couch near them.

There is a saying that I remember: "Great people talk about great ideas. Average people talk about things. Small people talk about other people." Moe's conversation always reflected the deep thinking of a great man.

Saturday morning, the children were anxious to go fishing. They were prepared and were waiting outside in the parking lot. It was a perfect morning to be outdoors.

The birds were chirping merrily in the trees. Nature was at peace with itself in such a tranquil environment. Years ago, these areas were devastated by the fury of Mother Nature.

Now the area had been restored. There was a calming effect resting over the area as if nature was at peace with itself. We drove to Moe's favorite fishing spot. The area was annihilated by the hurricane. Large trees had been uprooted and thrown in some other areas.

Trees were replanted by the county, but they were small compared to the massive ones that originally existed.

The river looked different from my previous visit. Everyone was armed with a fishing rod.

The American Dream

Puja said jokingly, "Let us have a fishing competition. My family against your family."

Moe's daughter added, "That is a brilliant idea."

With that spirited idea, the fishing became a serious sporting event. There is something about Naples that makes you forget all your troubles.

Is it the beautiful and scenic environment that makes us forget all our worries? Were these wondrous and picturesque places created to relax our body, mind, and spirit? My feelings were confirmed when I saw all the children enjoying their fishing competition.

There were six fishing rods, and everyone was reeling in fishes. There was an abundance of catches by Moe's family. At the end of the day, Team Moonan and family had caught more Bass fishes than Team Moe and family. Puja and Hema were very ecstatic when the result of the competition was announced by Moe.

That evening, we barbecued many fishes. Everyone enjoyed the feast. My family wanted to show our appreciation to our lovely hosts.

Hema said, "Daddy, can we make Chinese fried rice with shrimp and a nice potato salad for everyone for lunch tomorrow? Please, tell Moe's wife that we will cook on Sunday?"

"That is a good suggestion because they have to spend time taking care of the hotel," I added.

For the second consecutive night, my three daughters spent all night playing video games with Moe's children. They had put all their troubles behind for the present time.

My mind was in a state of happiness as I watched my children enjoying themselves. Their young innocent uncontrolled laughter made me realize that they needed my protection against a cruel world. I was their guardian and safe haven for my lifetime. The next day, Hema and I prepared a scrumptious Chinese meal, consisting of fried rice with shrimp and a potato salad. We made a drink from pineapple, mango, and milk. Puja spent time with Mala as we were cooking. Everyone enjoyed a hearty meal and complimented Hema's cooking.

The evening sun was sinking in the horizon. It was time to leave our faithful friends. We cried and hugged Moe's family and bade them farewell until another time. My three daughters were dead asleep in my new Toyota SUV. There is something about Naples that adds tranquility to your life. I drove into the beautiful sunset, heading for my home in Miami.

Omar Khayyam had said, "Your hands can seize today, but not tomorrow, and thoughts of your tomorrow are nothing but desire."

Plans are made for tomorrow, but time is the master of our destiny. Grasp every moment of life and enjoy it. No one can promise you better tomorrow.

CHAPTER ELEVEN

Strategy to Avoid Financial Disaster

After my rewarding visit to Naples, it was time to face reality. All my agonies following my divorce were behind me. The bridge of marriage had been burnt beyond repair. There was no turning back. My mind was now focused to meet my financial commitments and ensure my family was well cared for in my spare time.

Moe's advice to me was very simple: "You will need to get part-time employment at Hurts Rx drugstore for two nights weekly plus continue working at Sunset Pharmacy. Then you can spend the weekend with your daughters."

After one week of applying at Hurts Rx drugstore, my application was accepted for part-time work.

This was a great company with innovative ideas for increasing business. They were not family oriented like Sunset pharmacy. I missed the personal family touch that existed at Sunset pharmacy. The owner was always there with wise words of encouragements. My pharmacy in

Trinidad was managed with the same concept as Sunset Pharmacy.

Moe had said, "When it is possible on weekends to go on mini vacations with my children, my last advice to you, my friend, is to look after their spiritual edification. Get a place of worship for them. This is important like food for the soul. I have the name of a temple in Miami, and my friends there are Raj and Rita. When you have time, visit them soon."

Hema and Puja had heard about the Florida Keys from their schoolmates. They had spoken to me on a few occasions to visit this beautiful area. I wanted to surprise them for a weekend in the Keys for the Thanksgiving holidays. They were ecstatic about this trip.

The Florida Keys was my next stop. After working at both pharmacies for three months, my body was physically and mentally tired. My children needed a break from school to relax and enjoy the outdoors. Therefore, a visit to the Florida Keys was an ideal therapy for my three angels.

It provided some time to relax and enjoy with my family. According to the divorce documents, I had to get a written permission from my ex-wife, asking to take Mala to Key West. This was done one week before our journey to prevent any legal problems.

My girls were excited about this trip. We departed early on Saturday morning. The sun was now rising on the eastern skies. It was a perfect day for an outdoor adventure. My children were happy and excited about this journey. Hema and Puja had disagreements about who would be sitting in the front seat of the car. Both wanted the front seat for a better view and interfere with the music.

I told them that they have to learn to share and help each other in every way. When you learn to share as sisters, there will is a bond created that can never be destroyed. They decided mutually that they would sit alternately in the front seat and share in the music also.

A drive to the Keys is one of the most relaxing and exhilarating journey. It is one of the most beautiful places on this planet. This is Florida's Paradise. Our first stop was at Key Largo.

This area is breathtaking beautiful and so peaceful in the morning. The scenery is so tranquil. There is a calm and serenity that engulfs this place.

Hema complained, "Daddy, it is Thanksgiving, and we are hungry. Can we have breakfast at McDonald's? My belly is growling for food."

Everyone agreed that McDonald's was the ideal place for his or her Thanksgiving breakfast.

We agreed that this journey was not about rushing anywhere. It was a trip to relax the mind, body, and spirit. I was hoping to spend some quality time with my three angels.

My girls had a scrumptious breakfast of their choice. They were very happy. Puja was our professional photographer. Whenever we saw something beautiful or scenic, Puja would motion me to stop and take a lot of photographs. She was like a true professional, taking her job very seriously. Then we stopped at Islamorada. This was our first visit to the Keys.It was long overdue.

Again the scenery was utterly breathtaking. It was the most picturesque places in the world.

The crystal-clear waters gently caressed the white sandy shores. There were people fishing, boating, parasailing, fishing, and partying. It was lunchtime. Jose from Sunset Pharmacy had told me to stop and have lunch at Whale Harbor Restaurant in Islamorada.

He had said, trying to convince me, "My gosh, the food is so delicious at Whale Harbor! There is so much variety of foods. You must stop for lunch with your family. My whole family loves the buffet there. The ambience is out of this world. The dishes are mouth-watering.The restuarant overlooks the sea."

Mala looked tearful and said, "I am hungry and thirsty. Puja, can I have something to eat?"

We laughed because Mala never says she is hungry.

Puja added, "Yes, Daddy, my belly is grumbling. I am hungry too."

We reached Whale Harbor restaurant about noon. As Jose had said, The restaurant was situated snuggly, overlooking the ocean.

We got to sit at a table that overlooked the ocean. I kept Mala company, while Hema and Puja collected a lot of food. They brought three plates of food.

"Daddy, you know I am hungry," Mala repeated.

She was serious. She showed me her sad face. First and foremost, hungry Mala was served lunch. We ate ravenously. We ate from a wide range of sea foods—crabs, shrimps, fishes, and a wide array of other foods. Everyone was satisfied with the buffet. Our next stop was Marathon and the Lower Keys. We stopped frequently to admire nature at its best. On one occasion, we saw dolphins in their natural habitat, frolicking and playing and jumping out of the waters without a care in the world.

Mala was very amused to see them jumping and making funny noises.

She amusingly said, "Let us stay here forever. We can watch the dolphins. I love them. Can we catch one and take it back to the apartment, please? They are so pretty."

Hema hugged Mala and, laughing, added, "Mala, where are we going to put the dolphins?"

Mala's innocent reply was, "In my room, silly, in the bathtub. I will take care of it. I will feed it. He will be mine. Please, Daddy?"

Her pleading was very sincere and innocent. I lifted her and said, "You are going to make the parents cry if you take the babies. Next year, we are going to come back when the baby is grown up. Then we will catch him."

Puja and Hema were enjoying every moment of this playful conversation.

Puja jumped to add, "Remember, Daddy, you promised Mala you will catch one and put it in the bathtub next year. I am going to remind you next year."

My family was happy, and I did not feel any loneliness. Their joys, laughter, and happiness provided a blanket of comfort in my life. My father had told me, "When you have problems, there are two ways to distance yourself from it. First, find yourself in the company of children. Nothing troubles their innocent mind. Secondly, look to nature and stop to admire the moonlight or the vast ocean. Both are medications for the mind to forget all your troubles." He was so right. My three beautiful daughters buffered the effects of my loneliness. The Keys was like paradise. You can get lost in the panoramic beauty of this place. We had booked into a hotel near the beach. The sole purpose of choosing this location was that I wanted my children to witness the sunset with me.

Everyone changed hurriedly into their swimsuits, and we headed to the beach.

There was an unusual wailing sound coming from the beach. We saw a small crowd of people in the water. I placed Mala on my neck like a jockey on a horse, and we rushed in the direction of the crowd.

We were aghast with fear at what we were witnessing. Hema and Puja were crying. Mala could not understand what was unfolding before our eyes. She heard the pathetic sorrowful cry. At three years her age, she understood the language of sorrow.

My body trembled as I tried to comprehend the horrific scene unfolding in front of my eyes. Tears were streaming down my eyes. It was the most distressing sound as if something was dying. The white sands on the shores were bloodstained.

About a few hundred feet in front of us were about eight gigantic whales. These mammals are an endangered species, and everything must be done to save them. They were in distress and stranded in the shallow waters of the coral reefs.

The whales were crying as though they knew that death was imminent.

These magnificent creatures of the sea were stranded in the shallow waters of the reef. We rushed to help the other people that were providing assistance. Apparently, the whales were feeding and were swimming too close to the shores in high tide. However, they could not navigate back out from the shallow waters.

The cry of a whale in distress is heart-wrenching. All my daughters were crying. They watched the rescue effort from the safety of the shores. Close up to these magnificent creatures is a humbling experience.

To witness these mammals in danger gives you inner strength to save them. The water was about four feet deep. No one had the experience of saving a whale, but we knew that they had to get off the reef and into deeper waters.

As we pushed one of the whales away from the reef, blood flowed from a wound, sustained from the sharp corals. A loud wailing sound followed as he was freed from the coral.

We pushed the whale's fins, and the gigantic whale started to swim toward the deeper waters. The whale start to swim, then he stopped as though he was waiting for his friends.

Every time we pushed them into deeper waters, they swam back to their friends. It was a pitiful sight. Were they committing suicide, or were they a close-knit family that could not be separated?

We were happy to see the arrival of the Coast Guard boat. They were speeding in our direction. In a few minutes, like true saviors, they were in the water, fully equipped for a rescue effort. Everyone was clapping when they arrived, including little Mala.

We gladly assisted them as they directed us in this distressful situation. Six of the eight stranded whales were coerced into deep waters.

The remaining two whales were not so fortunate. They were washed ashore, bleeding profusely from wounds sustained on the coral reef. My daughters hugged the enormous giant of the sea and wept bitterly.

Their bodies were being tossed helplessly with each passing wave. There was a massive crowd that had gathered as the evening progressed into the late evening. The media was here, recording this pitiful sight.

The American Dream

The sun was sinking in the distant horizon. We did not notice the beautiful sunset. We departed to our hotel in a very depressed mood.

That day, I saw the human race working in collaboration with each other. There was no race or inequality, only people desperately trying to help a common rescue effort. No one mentioned black, white, or brown, only togetherness to help rescue the dying whale.

This is the passion that we must have for each other on a daily basis. This cooperation is lacking in the world. When anyone is in distress, we must jump in to assist, regardless of the problem. The world would be a better place if this were so. Jesus Christ said, "Love your neighbor as I have loved you"—great words of wisdom to follow from the Master. That night, everyone was sad and depressed. Mala asked the question, "Daddy, why am I so sad?" She jumped and sat on my lap. "Today, you witnessed something very sad. Yes, but we have to be thankful that at least six whales were saved. Mala, look at this rose. Is the rose pretty?"

"Yes," she said, reaching to take it from me. Her tender hand touched a thorn, and she said, "Ouch!"

I replied, "Then life is like a rose. The beauty and elegance is in the rose flower and the fragrance. Now look down lower. There are a dozen thorns. You touched a thorn, and it was a painful experience. Life is full of roses and thorns. We do not know when we will get a beautiful rose or confront many thorns in life.

We have to accept problems as they come, and sometimes, we have no control over them. You all are fortunate. You all are lucky. We protect you against the thorns of life. Look at the whale today. No one was there to protect them from the thorns of life. One of the reasons that we have each other is so we can help with the thorns of life."

Puja added, "Today, I realize that life is precious and that we have to protect it with all our strength. Today is a day to give thanks for life."

Hema was in deep thought. "Who protects these beautiful mammals of the seas? I am sure no one is doing that, and they are at the mercy of man and nature. Today, I am thankful so many people came to help the stranded whales. There should be a world wide effort to protect these magnificent mammals of the seas.If this not implemented, future generations will never enjoy their grace and beauty."

She was so correct in her assessment of these enormous creatures of the seas.

They are at the mercy of mankind and his vicious and selfless ways.

Sunday passed quietly without any unforeseen event. At lunchtime, we had turkey and all the trimmings that go with it. We spent the day basking in the sun and enjoying paradise. In the evening, we relaxed by the beach and witnessed the sun sinking in the ocean. This is the most astonishing view. The sun rays gently caresses the waves like the waves and the sun are united. The sun's rays penetrated the few clouds in the sky, causing a silver-lining effect.

Like the silver lining in the clouds, I wonder whether mankind will step up and provide laws and protection for these endangered species. There is a feeling of warmth and peace of mind that radiates from your heart when you witness the sunset from the Florida Keys.

Our journey homeward had begun. Everyone was exhausted. That familiar snoring sound was an indication that my daughters were in deep sleep.

As my children fell asleep, my mind was busy with many questions. Should I start dating or have a serious relationship now? Then I thought now was not the time; I needed to focus on spending more time with my daughters. What was needed for them was their spiritual edification.

Then a place of worship was what I needed to find on a Sunday. Hema and Puja were living full time with me; therefore, my duty to them was to play the role of father and mother. A decision had to be made whether to keep both jobs in the two pharmacies.

The two jobs were becoming very stressful. I could not risk physical and mental breakdown with the excessive amounts of extra hours that I was working. Jose had said indirectly that he wanted to sell the pharmacy. My best choice, though not the wiser one, was to work full time at Hurts Rx drugstore.

The best choice was to give Jose enough notice so that he was not upset that I was leaving his pharmacy. I wanted to inform in advance. Hurts Rx drugstore had promised me full-time work.

Changes in life are inevitable. We have to learn to adapt and move on.

Anyone who has been through a divorce will understand that it is like getting stabbed in your back. It is a traumatic experience. Life goes on, when bridges are burnt under your feet. Do not look back; instead, try to build a new life.

It is not easy task. It is like starting all over again. Life is an evolving process. We have to adapt and move on. I promised that I would not have any serious personal relationship for some time. I needed to search to find myself. I wanted to build a solid relationship with my

THE AMERICAN DREAM

children. Puja was interested in continuing her dance classes here.

My mind was busy with so many plans to continue a new life.

On Thanksgiving, there was so much to be thankful to since coming to the United States.

We have a few faithful friends. We were then slowly creeping toward the American dream. My first stop was to my ex-wife's home. Mala had fallen asleep as I handed her to her mother. I kissed Mala good-bye until my next allocated visit on the weekend.

There were two important missions my family had to accomplish by the end of the year.

As a family, we had to return to Trinidad to renew our work permit with the United States Embassy in Port of Spain. I decided that I would work extra hours to save money for our trip to Trinidad. We were anxiously looking forward to this vacation because I had not seen my family in two years.

For the next two months, all the money that I earned from my extra hours was focused on paying on court order and saving money for our vacation. Hema and Puja were capable of handling all the household duties, while I concentrated on working the grave shift. My birthday is in November.

My son told me on the phone, "Daddy, do not celebrate your birthday. When you come to Trinidad, we will have a big party."

According to my divorce documents, if I was to leave the country with Mala, then I had to obtain written permission from her mother. This was accomplished quickly. Now, we looked forward for two weeks of leisure time in Trinidad.

CHAPTER TWELVE

Journey to Roots

Our journey to Trinidad was a welcome one. On one hand, we had not seen our family for the past two years. On the other hand, in order to relax, my children needed a break from school and, in my daughters' words, "the pressures of life."

It is important that my children know their roots to maintain an identity of their birthplace. It is a fact that to move on in life, you must learn about your roots.

On our last flight from Trinidad to Miami, we traveled on American Airlines. This time around, we booked on Caribbean Airlines to Trinidad. The flight was smooth and without any incidents.

We cleared customs and hurriedly exited the airport. A group of family members was anxiously awaiting our arrival.

"Oh my goodness! There is our family!" I said to Hema and Puja in a joyous mood. My eldest sister grabbed Mala and gave her a kiss.

My father and mother were the first ones to greet me.

With clasped hands, I greeted them "Jai Sita Ram" and touched their feet as a mark of respect and love for my parents.

My son, Jewan, was standing patiently beside them. He hugged me tightly like a long-lost friend.

All my brothers and sisters were there to greet us. There were a lot of hugs and kisses flowing around. Tears flowed freely from my family. They had missed our presence immensely.

My three daughters and I were welcomed as if royalty had arrived in the airport. Mala was tossed from hand to hand; everyone wanted to hug her and pinch her cute cheeks.

We felt special and fortunate to receive such a warm reception. All the neighbors also were there. This type of reception reminded me of the times when I was a young boy.

There was so much joy and love that I missed the attention and comfort that flowed from my family. Even as an adult, I missed the love and protection that my family and friends showed to me. As we reached my parents' home, there was a big reception awaiting us. There was even a larger crowd at my parents' room than at the airport.

My daughters were really touched by the love that flowed naturally from the hearts of our forgotten friends and family. For the last two years, I had neglected to just pick up the telephone and give a friendly greeting. In my heart, I felt guilty that I did not communicate with my close friends. Their welcoming smiles warmed my guilty heart.

Everyone had join together to prepare a variety of exotic dishes. There were so many different foods that I had not eaten since my absence from Trinidad. It was a joyous and gluttonous time. For the next two weeks, my daughters and I were pampered and treated like royalty.

It was as if a long-lost family had found its way home. Some of my daughters' friends were there to welcome them. My father summoned us to sit and enjoy the buffet-style meal.

He hugged me and said, "Welcome back, beta (or, my son). Right now, let us eat. I am sure everyone is extremely hungry. We have two weeks to enjoy your company."

With that short speech, we started an hour-long feast. My daughters were lost in conversation with their friends. I was wedged between my mother and my son. Everyone was talking and eating at the same time.

A handful of my friends from my Hindu school and my pharmacy in Trinidad were here. My son Jewan had organized this reception. I was proud that he had organized such a heartfelt welcome. No one moved from their tables, and the conversation continued for two hours.

My father interjected, "Moonan, carry your bags to the rooms upstairs. Organize a room for my granddaughters next to yours. Jewan will help you."

With that gentle command, we proceeded upstairs to organize our rooms. Jewan touched my shoulder and said, "Dad, look at the breathtaking view of the Caroni Plains that you always talk about."

I turned to look at a view of Caroni that relaxed my mind over the years. "Wow! It is picturesque and tranquil as if I left it only yesterday" was my pleasant response.

My daughters were staring at the panoramic view of the mountains and the undulating plains. They were awed by the beauty of the picturesque scenery. It was unchanged in its beauty and splendor.

After a few hours, I finally found time to have a heart-to-heart talk with my son. Jewan motioned me to walk to the banks of the Caroni River. As we walked toward the banks of the Caroni River,

I was at a loss for words to say to him. There were so many things that I wanted to tell him that they stifled

The American Dream

my mind. I put my hand on his shoulder, and we walked towards our destination.

I said sadly, "Son, I missed you a lot. Every day I would think about you. "Then we saw my dad running toward us, so we stopped walking.

My father caught up with us and said, "Guys, you have a party in your honor. You cannot leave your guest and walk out of the party. You must come back immediately. I know you want to talk privately with your son, but now is not the time for it."

With that command, we proceeded back to the party. He was correct in his assessment of the situation. We were being very selfish. They had planned a program, so it was time for speech making. My dad was the first one to volunteer to give a speech.

He started, "When my son left here two years ago, I thought that I would never see him again. Today, my heart is filled with joy and satisfaction to see you in our presence. I missed you, my son.

A lot of people from this area have left Trinidad, but they never returned to their roots. Today, I am proud that you stand in front of me. I know you are a fighter, and nothing discourages you. I see fire and determination in your eyes to achieve your goals. You are a true Baijoo.

I know that you will make us proud. Your mother is too emotional to say anything, but she welcomes you with all her heart. Here is to Moonan, and may he conquer the American dream."

There was laughter and applause from the gathering. I reached and hugged my parents, with my heart filled with emotions. I looked at them and saw tears streaming down their eyes.

My father is a strong man physically, but he is very sentimental. I remembered him saying once, "Shedding tears does not show any weakness. In fact, it shows your strength. Look in the Bible.

It says that Jesus Christ wept openly. Tears are not only for sorrows but also to show your happiness. To show that you are strong, sometimes tears help in certain situations."

My son Jewan was summoned to give a speech. His friends applauded as he stood up. "It is difficult not having my father at this stage in my life. However, I think of the good times that we had, and I am happy. My studies keep my mind occupied. I miss playing tennis and cricket with him."

He walked up to me and hugged me. There was a loud round of applause for my son's short but emotional speech.

One of my brothers added, "On Sunday, we have a cricket match. Father and son will open the game, and that is Jewan and Moonan. Be ready to play a good game."

I interjected, "Oh, that is great. It will be just like the old times." My eldest brother interrupted with a glass in hand, and I believe a bit intoxicated, "I want all of you to know that I was Moonan's teacher in Mathematics.

He had failed this subject in high school, and I taught him at home every evening. I missed him here because he was my pharmacist and still my dearest brother. Cheers to your family."

He raised his glass to toast for our good health. Everyone was talking about the positive side of my life. I was glad that no one was dwelling on the negative aspects of my life. One of my sisters wanted to give a speech.

With a glass of wine in her hand, she started to say, "I have never seen so much competition in a family to be the best like the Baijoo brothers.

They have competition to be the best in fishing or swimming and even the best in playing cards. I know it is all in fun. I know they miss you, Moonan.

I worked with you in your pharmacy, and I am glad that I spent time with you. We all love you and your family.

Whether you are here or abroad, you will always be a part of the Baijoo extended family. Thank you."

My other brother continued, "What about cooking? Moonan cannot cook a good meal like me."

I replied jokingly, "Yes, Brother, you are right. Your food tastes better than mine." Everyone was joking and enjoying the evening. The music of Trinidad chutney and calypso were being blasted loudly, and my daughters were dancing with their friends. Mala was in the centre of the dance floor with the others.

One of my brothers announced, "Guys, you all should get some rest because tomorrow morning, we are taking you all to Caura River." The partying and dancing continued until two in the morning.

Everyone was tired but were enjoying themselves. No one wanted to go to sleep because the party and friends were enjoyable.We slept for about three hours. We were headed for Caura River by eight in the morning. We had in our company about forty family members and friends.

The drive to Caura River was one of the most scenic in Trinidad. The tranquil gentle breeze caressed our body as we drove carefully up the winding mountainous roads. The view of the Central Range was breathtaking. As we drove toward our destination, the road meandered dangerously close to the precipice.

A multitude of colorful trees adorned the roadsides. The trees were swaying gently in the air-conditioned mountain breeze. As we ascended into the mountains, a feeling of tranquility engulfed my body.

My father was right in asking to look to nature for relaxation and comfort. My son was my chauffeur. My daughters were dispersed in the other cars accompanying us. In his vehicle, Jewan was joined by three of his friends from his university. Jewan introduced me to them, and he proceeded to talk about his university studies.

Jewan moanfully added, "The most difficult time of my life is at the university. You have to study all day and night to pass one tedious exam. Then you have to be extremely consistent. You cannot get sick or depressed. It is an everyday challenge for four years."

His friend cheerfully added, "Yes, it is difficult, man. Our university is the most difficult in the world to make the grades."

I interrupted his conversation, "You guys have it easy today. Count your blessings. When I went to this university, it was more difficult than for you guys."

I stopped talking to see if they were curious about what I was talking.

Jewan added, "Daddy, please let us about your experiences. My friends will get a kick out of it."

I added, "My family could not afford my university tuition fees. Therefore, I had to work for one year in order to save my money. After this time, I was able to apply to our university for admittance. Apart from my job and studies, I had to help my family on the weekends in the sugarcane fields and rice fields. You know my brothers and sisters also helped my parents when they were not working"

Jewan's friend blurted out, saying, "Uncle, you are joking. Are you not? Jewan said that you like to joke a lot."

"No, no, young man," I added, "on the contrary, it is true. Consider what wages laborers made from the sugar estates. My parents were paid minimal wages by their British colonial masters.

After Trinidad and Tobago won independence, the wages were slightly better, but my parents were still very poor. They worked seven days a week just to support their family with the bare necessities for survival.

I have seen the Caroni River overflow its banks and destroy most of my family possessions. Now do you think that my father could have afforded university tuition fees?

The American Dream

Taking a student loan was out of the question because they required a security deposit which too was out of the question. However, nothing was going to deter my ambition of becoming a doctor or a pharmacist.

I had the motivation and the qualifications to attend a university, but no finance was available. My parents were the ones to push into my head that I must get a college degree, but there was no money.

Therefore, I worked for one year and saved my money. At university, I continued working at least forty hours weekly at Ross drugstore to pay my bills. I was never upset with my parents for not being able to afford my tuition fees. Instead, my heart sympathized with their plight.

As children, we tend to blame parents for everything. That is totally wrong. Sometimes, we have to battle for ourselves. When we battle for yourself, the satisfaction and accomplishment are greater in the end."

Jewan's friend humbly added, "You know that I have never worked a day in my life. I do not know what work is all about. My parents are filthy rich, so my life is definitely more different than yours by a mile."

I interrupted him, saying, "On the contrary, my humble upbringing helped me survive the first two years in Florida. When I reached there, nothing worked in my favor, but I was not discouraged easily. My parents' status here made me stronger to cope with any problems that the world tossed in my direction."

The journey to Caura River lasted about one hour. Jewan and I were able to get acquainted with some things from the past two years. It was a relaxing conversation that made the time flew quickly by. We had reached our destination by ten o'clock.

My brother added, "We have to reach early otherwise the good camping sites for cooking and camping will be occupied."

As we exited from the vehicles, I realized that we had driven high inside the mountains. We were surrounded by huge bamboo trees. The car park was on high land.

We had to descend a steep gravel road to reach the crystal-clear stream was hidden deep within two valleys. This is one of nature's wonders in Trinidad, discreetly hidden in the beautiful mountainside.

My daughters dived into the cool clear waters. I joined in their frolicking. The waters had a calming yet invigorating effect on my body. About thirty family members had joined us in the water. They started a friendly water fight. Everyone was splashing water on each other.

Again, there was going to be another party with music, dance, and cooking. Everyone were in a festive mood. My brothers were looking for dry bamboo to light a fire to cook the food.

Everyone helped organize the music that was being played very loudly. My eldest sister started to dance to the music and summoned my three daughters to join her. They gladly obliged and joined her in the merrymaking. With the assistance of his machete and bamboo sticks,one of my brother made some makeshift benches for sitting.

From the previous night, the party continued throughout the evening by the Caura River. Every so often, someone was offering some delicacy to eat which I never had for the last two years. I had acquired the taste for American food, but I missed the Trinidadian cuisine. The festivities continued until seven o'clock when mosquito bites ended the festivities.

The closeness and the bond that existed with my family were rekindled. Two years of separation was not enough to destroy our mutual love. My family spoke to me as if there was no separation between us.

My sister said, "When people returned from United States, they talk about that country as though it is El

Dorado. You know the lost city where everything is gold and everything is perfect. Is your story like that?"

She looked at me with piercing eyes. I laughed and hugged her tightly.

Our relaxing day had unfortunately come to an end.

Then we journeyed back to my parents' home. There was silence in the car as we drove back home. My stories were not like El dorado, but I was not going to burden my family with distressing news. My divorce was the only bad news that they spoke frequently.

My father said bluntly, "Tragedyt happens. Life goes on. Do not let my grandchildren suffer for other people's mistakes. They did not ask to come in this world."

We headed in the darkness to our home in Caroni Village. Everyone was exhausted and retired early to bed. The next day was a big day. My brothers had planned a cricket match. It was going to be another day of partying and enjoyment.

Sunday morning, about forty family or friends had gathered at the Caroni Hindu School playground for another day of fun. This time, it was for a friendly cricket match. Fond memories of my childhood flashed across my mind.

On this playground, I played football barefooted in the rain. All the laughter and sorrows rushed across my mind as if it happened only yesterday. It was embedded in my memory as a lighthouse erected in the sea of time.

As we journeyed past that lighthouse, every moment came back so vividly. At this school, I was taught, "Knowledge is power. Education is not just learning in school but absorbing everything positive from life and applying it to everyday situations." I remembered their teachings: "God is one. Truth is one. Wise men call him by many names." Then I felt a thud on my shoulder. "Daddy, are you daydreaming?" Jewan asked me.

"Yes, this place will always be in my heart. This school molded me to be a strong person. They taught me to be meek but strong. Ah, so good memories" I said in a very emotional tone.

The weather was cooperating to give us a beautiful sunny day. It was a perfect day for a game of cricket. Again food, drinks, and music accompanied this game. It was billed as a day of fun, but every player was serious and focused in playing their best that day.

The Baijoo family played this game regularly. Our family had won many tournaments and trophies. Even as a pharmacist, there was cricket competition against different professional organizations like doctors and dentists for charities. Cricket, like baseball, has two opposing sides.

A home run in baseball is counted as six runs in cricket. Unlike baseball, there are two batsmen in the game at one time. That day's game was Baijoo's family versus Baijoo's friends. Team Baijoo was made up of my brothers, sisters, and my daughters.

Team Baijoo elected to bat. My eldest brother summoned my son and me to bat in the opening. Jewan faced the first ball of the innings. With lighting speed, the bowler came from the other end. Jewan slammed the ball over the boundary for six runs or a home run. The crowd went wild with joy. Everyone was clapping. Next ball was given the same treatment, another home run.

Jewan repeated this three times in the six balls bowled to him. Now was my turn to bat. The crowd was silent as the bowler came thundering down. I flashed my bat with all my strength and the ball went shooting over the boundary.

I smiled broadly as I smashed my first home run. Father and son team aggravated fifty runs, then I was given out. My brother came and was striking the ball boundary after boundary. My eldest sister hit a home run too.

Everyone, including Hema and Puja, made some runs. At the end of our innings, we had scored two hundred runs.

The American Dream

Everyone was clapping with the high score of team Baijoo. It was lunchtime. My sisters had made their famous roti and chicken for lunch. Both teams sat together like friends and shared their prepared food.

Our disc jockey was there entertaining us with the latest songs. Mala was in the care of some mothers who had children about her age. Mala was dancing to the music.

Everyone was ready to begin the second innings. Now, Team Baijoo was fielding. The opposing team was batting. My brother was bowling the first ball of the game. He came thundering down toward the batsman.

The ball hit the wicket, and the first player had strike out. The crowd invaded the field in a joyous mood. The next player came and prepared to bat. Again, my brother was right on target—a second strikeout in two balls.

Again, the crowd interrupted the game. There was thunderous applause as my brother repeated the third strikeout in one over. Jewan was given the ball, and he came in full speed toward the batsman. The ball was driven straight to my sister, and she caught it. The umpire gave the batsman out.

The crowd went wild with jubilation. With each successive ball, Team Baijoo was moving toward victory.

Like a lion stalking its prey, Team Baijoo did not relent. At the end, victory belonged to Team Baijoo.

We devoured the other team. The partying continued until the evening.

The sun was kissing the horizon as it bade good-bye for another day. Everyone stayed and joked about a fantastic victory. My parents were particularly proud of Team Baijoo. Everyone departed as it was getting dark. Jewan and I decided to walk back home.

We finally had some quality time to reacquaint ourselves for the last two years. At my parents' home, everyone was awaiting our return. In the morning, we had to go to the United States Embassy to renew our visas.

We arrived at the Embassy very early in the morning. We completed the process in a short time. The consular said that our passports would be mailed in a few days.

Jewan and my daughters headed for Maracas Beach to relax for the day. The winding roadway was dangerous, but my son maneuvered cautiously through the narrow mountains.

Maracas Bay is a serene world by itself. It lies secluded behind the mountains.

The American Dream

The world would seem to stand still as you enter this beautiful area. This area has a special meal. It is the world famous bake and shark. Visitors come from all over the world to taste this bake and shark menu.

We sat and enjoyed a full meal. Then we proceeded to enjoy the blue, clear waters of Maracas Beach. We lay basking in the white sands as my children built sand castles. As I looked at my family enjoying themselves without a care in the world, I promised myself that I would take care of them through thick and thin. Jewan and I spoke about everything.

When life is tough, these precious moments make life worth living. We headed for another round of bake and shark before proceeding to our parents home. Everyone was extremely exhausted on our journey homeward.

My father was waiting anxiously in the front yard. He was waiting to tell my daughters a true story. My daughters were rested from their sleep in the car.

It was customary that my parents would sit at nights and tell all these incredible stories. There were many of the neighbors' children sitting anxiously to hear that night's story.

My father started speaking very softly, "Tonight, I am not going to tell you stories of kings, queens, or princess but of a true story that happened in Trinidad."

Journey of an Immigrant

He paused to drink some water. Everyone was very quiet. You could have heard a pin drop. He continued, "This is my favorite story. It is true. One day, before you return to Florida, you must visit this wonder that was built. It is the struggle of one man against nature and the unfair practices of the British Government.

His name was Bhai Sewdass Sadhu. He was brought from India as a poor indentured laborer or slave to work on the British sugar plantation or fields. He was born in Benares, India, on the banks of the Ganges River.

The British did not allow the Indians to build Hindu temples or a place to worship on their land even if the land was useless. The idea was that the Indians, without a place to worship, would eventually convert to Christianity.

However, Sadhu decided in his spare time to build a temple by the sea. The land he chose for the temple site was swampy land that borders the seashore. This land was useless to his British masters.

He used a bicycle to transport the materials that he needed for his planned project. He carried two buckets on the handlebars. On one bucket, he carried cement and, on the other side, gravel.

After years of physical and financial sacrifice, a beautiful temple emerged from the swampy wasteland. He had built his temple on the seashore. This was his temple on the banks of his Ganges in Trinidad. He planted many different flowers all around the temple. People came from afar to worship or just to view such an incredible feat of one man. In 1930, the British noticed the building. They asked him to destroy the temple.

He refused on grounds that he could not desecrate a temple. He said that was holy grounds. He was taken to court and fined five hundred dollars. In those days, that was a lot of money.

He had to pay this money in installments from his meagerly income. In addition, he was imprisoned for fourteen days. The British demolished the temple. They had no use for the land.

After he was released from prison, he started to build a temple inside the sea. He began the laborious work when the sea tide was low. With his bicycle, he carried gravel and cement every day for years until a magnificent temple emerged from the waters. You see, my children, anything is possible.

You have to focus and sacrifice to accomplish great things in life. With God, anything is possible. Always pray—God is waiting to listen to you. Shree Sadhu died in 1970. Over the years, the temple was reinforced and restored to a wondrous beauty. Today, it stands as a symbol of beauty and commitment for a man who dedicated his life so others may benefit from his sacrifice.

"A statue stands at the entrance of the temple of Shri Sewdass Sadhu. He stands as if he is welcoming everyone. Children, when you put your mind, you can achieve the greatest. He left his legacy in this world. Shri Sadhu was not a living dead. In school, if you strive for excellence, the rewards will be great. Now it is time for questions."

Mala raised her hand and said, "Nana (or Grandpa), can I go and see the temple in the sea, or was it a story?"

"You sure will. Jewan is going to take you when he has time, and my sweet angel, the story is true" answered my father with a broad smile.

One of the neighbors' children asked a question. "Grandpa, can anyone visit the temple?" My father was quick to answer because the child was of Muslim background.

"Sadhu built the temple for all to come and worship or just to enjoy the beauty of the surroundings. It was not made for any particular religion, creed, or race."

Hema asked her Nana, "Did Sadhu ever return to India? "Grandpa said, "Yes, he did, but the money he made from working could not afford his regular visits. When he could not visit his Ganges in India, he decided to build his temple near the sea like the Ganges."

Puja said, "Grandfather, are you going with us? Please come?" Her Grandfather smiled and said, "Yes, I have one request—that Nani (or Grandma) come with us." Grandma smiled and said that she will go.

After a wonderful story, ice cream was served to his listening audience.

The next day, we visited the temple by the sea. It was a wondrous sight. My father turned to my mother and said, "Now, I can die in peace. My eyes have seen what man can build for God. Now I want to see what God has built for me."

My mother showered the same sentiments like her husband. Their destiny was with God. My parents beckoned me to the shores of the magnificent temple.

With tears in my mother's eyes she said,

"Beta meaning son in Hindi. Trinidad is your roots. This land is sacred to you. This is where your journey in life begins. Do not forget your roots. A tree without root cannot survive. Our roots are in India. One day, I want you to make that journey for papa and myself. If we are alive then we want to know about India. One day make that sacred journey for us".

I hugged my parents and promised them that one day, I will visit Bihar in India. This is where the Baijoo journey began. This will be certainly a very emotional journey.

We watched the sun sinking into the sea against the backdrop of the temple. Now, everyone saw the beauty of the temple as Sadhu envisioned it. This was truly a sentimental and emotional sight. Listening to the story and then visiting the site brings tears to the most stubborn person. The next day, my parents had a puja (or prayer) for my family.

For the remaining days of our vacation, we would visit friends and families. We made trips to the Caroni Bird Sanctuary, the Toco lighthouse, fishing in the Caroni River, and many beaches.

Now, it was the night before our return to Florida. This night was going to be very sentimental and emotional. My son had organized my belated birthday party combined with a farewell party. All well wishers had gathered at my brother's home to bade us a happy trip and farewell until we return to Trinidad.

I stood and said my farewell speech, "My parents were not rich materially, but they taught us how to love and be contented.

The essence of life is living in harmony with each other. Loving and helping people is what makes us humans. I am thankful that my family treats me like a king. God bless you all. For two weeks, we were pampered like babies.

I will never forget my roots and the people here who love my family so much like their own flesh and blood. We love you all. We will miss you all dearly."

Everyone was in tears as I took turns in hugging all my friends, neighbors, and family.

The next day, Jewan drove us to the airport. It was a sad farewell from my family. My son spent time with us at the airport. We hugged and shed tears. Then we departed through Immigration. In four hours, we had landed in Miami.

Our journey to our roots will live vividly in our hearts and minds for a long time.

CHAPTER THIRTEEN

Adaptation to Changes

This day was a new chapter in my life. It was time for change and drastic decisions.

Changes in life are inevitable. Human beings do not like many changes in their lives. Everyone likes his or her comfort zone, with no drastic changes. However, Mother Nature shows that to survive, changes are inevitable. The night changes to day and back again. The season and weather changes.

That day was my first day at Sunset Pharmacy after my journey to my roots.

Dr. Maria and I had private decisions about my resignation from Sunset Pharmacy. As I entered the pharmacy, I took a deep breath to relax myself. Jose entered the pharmacy.

He rushed to hug me and said, "My long-lost friend, how was your vacation? I missed you so much. The pharmacy was in chaos without you. I am glad you are back to work. Please come to my office. Do you want some Cuban coffee?"

He motioned me to his office where Dr. Maria was already sitting. I reached and hugged her as if she was my mother. She was strangely silent.

Jose started to say, "Both of you are important to me. I am going to inform you what is happening with my pharmacy. Two large pharmacy chain stores are bidding to buy my pharmacy immediately. They have promised to keep all the workers here.

"They have offered me five times what my pharmacy is worth in my stock. One day, there will be no mom and dad business in the United States because big companies are swallowing up all the small business. There are no laws to protect the small fishes in the big ocean of business.

For example, big chain pharmacies offer a twenty-five-dollar gift card for transferring one prescription for aspirin to a patient. Can I compete with that? I have to sell or move to a location far from this one.

The bidders for my pharmacy said that they need both of you here working for them. I am sorry, but this is the end of the road for me. My decision may be selfish, but I need your support."

Jose was close to tears. Dr. Maria had worked for him for twenty years. Dr. Maria was weeping bitterly. I reached for her hand, and she turned and hugged me. She remained silent.

Now was the time for my resignation news. "Both of you were my first true Hispanic family in the United States. Dr. Maria, you treated me like your son. Thank you for everything, but I cannot work for you anymore. Here is my letter of resignation. I will never forget your kindness."

Dr. Maria wiped her teary eyes and said, "I am traumatized twice in one day. Jose, do you know what large companies do when they buy small pharmacies like yours? Two months after they purchase the company, all the employees are laid off. It is called downsizing. I am sixty-two years of age.

Do you think a new company will want an old lady working for them? On the contrary, they will hire a new graduate in my position. They will pay him less salary for the same work. They do not care about experience or your length of service. Most of my workers here do not speak English.

Do you think a big company will tolerate that? Moonan, I wish you the best, and do not forget me. Moonan, you are not *like* my son. You *are* my son."

Jose started crying. He rushed out of his office. That would be the last time that I would see Jose again. He never returned any of my numerous telephone calls. Everyone felt that this drastic decision to sell his beloved pharmacy made him live a secluded life.

As Dr. Maria and I returned to the pharmacy, all the workers had gathered together to say their last farewell. Jose had hurriedly departed from his office. One of the workers said that he had sold his soul to the devil in the sale of his loved possession.

This pharmacy proved to be my savior in the most depressing time of my life. My memories of this place was pleasant and rewarding. I felt depressed that I was deserting the pharmacy that treated me like a family. Changes in life are inevitable. Sometimes, drastic decisions are necessary to prevent impending disaster.

This pharmacy was being sold; therefore, the new owners may not rehire me. As I departed from the pharmacy, tears came to my eyes. This was the pharmacy where I walked to work, then rode my bicycle to reach here.

I looked at the road where my feet walked many miles to my beloved pharmacy. My father's advice was, "Do not forget those who helped you along the road to your success. Keep the line of communication open."

One month later, I visited Sunset Pharmacy. There was no sign in front of the pharmacy. The doors were locked with chains. On looking inside, the building was vacant. A big corporation had bought the pharmacy because it posed a threat to the profits of their nearby store.

Later, Dr. Maria told me that none of the workers were rehired. She was taking a long vacation to relax her mind and comprehend the trauma that unfolded. She was traveling to India for five weeks.

My new job was full time at Hurts Rx Pharmacy.

I missed my friends at Sunset pharmacy.Dr.Maria and Jose provided friendliness that is the essence of pharmacy service. The friendly laughter that was the keystone to the success of Sunset Pharmacy resonated in my mind.

Working full time was depressing. After my shift, I reached my apartment to see Puja in a very depressed mood. This was unlike her countenance. She is always pleasant and fun-loving.

Puja had finished high school with honors. Her GPA was above four. She could not get a scholarship because she was not an American citizen.

"Daddy, life is not fair. I achieved better grades than all my friends in my class. However, everyone received

The American Dream

a scholarship because of their race or background. How unlucky can I be?

Why was there no scholarship for someone with excellent grades? I came to this country legally. Then why was I not given a full scholarship?"

With that emotional outburst, Puja broken down and cried uncontrollably. She asked an important question. Why was a scholarship given on the basis of race? That kind of scholarship is good.

However, scholarships should also be given for students with excellent grades, who are legally in this country. The criteria for scholarships should be primarily excellent grades.

"The solution, my dear, is to focus on achieving good grades. Someone at university level will recognize your achievements and reward you eventually. Do not worry, you will always have my support. I will sacrifice so that you will achieve your dreams."

Puja answered half-heartedly, but I understood her sentiments, "I guess, but it is not right in any way. Life is unfair. "With that statement, Puja dismissed that subject, and she never mentioned it again.

For her high school graduation, I bought a used Honda Civic motorcar. She was extremely happy. She applied to

FIU, and her application was accepted. My daughter was now attending college. Her dreams of becoming a nurse were in the horizon.

Like the Florida weather that changes very fast, my life was changing at a fast pace. One day my ex wife Sandra made an emotional telephone call saying "you have to take custody of Mala, my job requires that I work varying hours, therefore it's impossible to send her to school on a regular basis

For a moment, I reflected on what my mother had said: "Do not abandon your children. They are your wealth."

I had no girlfriend to help with Mala, so I became both mother and father to my daughters. With that simple request, the court gave me custody of Mala.

My family was growing. One day, Hema suggested, "Daddy, you are paying a high rent for this apartment. Why don't you save some money and make a down payment on a house?"

But I had no savings. That would mean working extra works to get the down payment. "It is a fantastic idea" was my zestful answer.

Hema continued with a smile, "I have a plan. Puja and I will take care of Mala. You can work extra hours at the pharmacy. You can take care of Mala when you are home."

The American Dream

With that plan of action, I worked the night shift for five days a week. As my friend Moe had said, "You need to leave the weekend free to spend time with your family."

Hema, Puja, and I alternated our schedule so that we spent all our free time with Mala.

Baby Mala was growing into a beautiful princess. She was attending school and singing the alphabet.

After six months of sacrifice, I had saved enough money to pay a deposit on my dream home.

After looking diligently for another six months, we bought a house in South Dade. The house was in a very dilapidated condition. However, with extra work, it would become a thing of beauty.

The location was ideal. It was near FIU and the Florida Turnpike. The surrounding environment was quiet and tranquil. The house was located away from the loud traffic.

Many repairs was necessary to bring the structure to a comfortable standard of living.

My plan was to continue renting the apartment for one month. After one month of continuous work, the house was brought to a reasonable standard of living.

Within a few months of moving into our new home, we felt the ungodly wrath of Hurricane Wilma and Katrina. Disaster hit hard with all its fury. Our home sustained extensive damage.

Our roof was leaking. Parts of our massive avocado trees were thrown on the rooftop. The raging winds tossed our garage into the neighbor's lawn. The adjoining fence was ripped to shreds.

My newly planted fruit trees were flattened to the ground. Our beautiful flowers that we had patiently planted had been decimated. They were uprooted as if someone had dug them out.

The neighborhood was like a disaster zone. There was no electricity for about two weeks. The whole neighborhood looked dismembered like a disaster area. Every household in our area suffered extensive damage.

Hema and Puja came to me with a brilliant idea, saying, "Daddy, why don't you cook all the food in the fridge and share it with the neighbors? It will spoil anyway. Besides, no one has power to cook food. We know how to make a fireside like in Trinidad."

A fireside is made using four bricks to hold up the large pot and then wood is used for fuel. We used all the shattered wood thrown all over the lawns as firewood.

Within two hours, we were sharing our famous *pelau* recipe in the neighborhood.

The next evening, we cooked again and shared with our new friends. This catastrophe had brought the neighborhood closer together. Everyone was sharing. We took turns clearing trees and debris from everyone's property. My father had told me,

"Sometimes, God wakes up people with disasters. It brings us closer together. The essence of survival is to help each other. Your neighbor is your friend and extended family."

For the next week, my family knew everyone in the surroundings. There was so much love and caring. My family had survived two major hurricanes in a short space of time. Life must go on.

We picked up the pieces and moved on with our lives. After a short time, we sacrificed and worked day and night to restore our little dream home. Since coming to Florida in the search for material gains, I had neglected the spiritual needs of my family. In my journey to my roots, my mother had vehemently told me, "Son, your children are like seedlings.

They must be nurtured in the right way. You must feed equally their physical, mental, and spiritual needs. Soak their roots with love. "After the hurricanes, my family searched online to find a Hindu temple in the vicinity of our home.

It was like trying to find a needle in a haystack. For a large population in Miami, there were hardly any followers of Hinduism here. However, we found a small but friendly temple on the South Dixie Highway.

My daughters found a small but welcoming environment in this temple. Hema and Puja started dance classes at the temple. The pundit (or priest) was originally from Guyana.

With clasped hands, he welcomed us to his humble place of worship, saying, "Namaste, Bhai, swaagatam." (Meaning, "Brother, I welcome you in the name of God.") "My name is Rajesh. Everyone calls me Raj. This temple belongs to everyone, so make good use of its facilities.

This is a place of enlightenment. This is a place where God takes care of your troubles. We are here to help you in whatever way possible. Here is my cell phone number. You can call me 24x7."

He had a pleasant outlook as if he was at peace with the world. This pundit preached universal love and understanding. He continued, "In life, you have to be very practical. I can speak Spanish fluently because the majority of people here speak that language. Adaptation, my brother, is the key to survival. My education was in India. I can speak Hindi, Sanskrit, and a little Urdu. Do you want to improve your life? Then learn like Gandhi to accept all teachings. Only then you can become an enlightened soul."

Raj showed the relevance of scriptures written thousands of years ago in today's lifestyle.

He said, "All scriptures are inspiration of God—means all, whether it is Hinduism, Christianity, or Islam. The concept is the same. No true scriptures teach harm to anyone. True scriptures teach harmony with God and mankind."

His concept of life was similar to great saints like my teacher Sai Baba. From Trinidad, I followed Sai Baba teachings because he taught that all religions had the same concept.

My family would spend a lot of spare time with the members of the temple. Puja was zestful in joining their dance classes. Her closest friend there was Rita and her daughter, Mena. This family would be a source of comfort for my family. Rita would consider me her older brother. Puja was an avid dancer at Lakshmi Girls High School in Trinidad. This was my advice to her: "Puja, remember, your university studies are your priority. Do not lose sight of your goal."

She was adamant and said, "Daddy, let us make a deal. If my grades fall badly, then I am going to quit dancing."

With that friendly rebuttal to her father, Puja would go on to win many dance competitions. She spent the weekends dancing in temples and for charity events throughout Florida. At FIU, Puja achieved honors. I was ecstatic.

One day, in the quietness of my bedroom, my three daughters knocked on the door. They all jumped on my bed and made themselves comfortable.

I asked them, "Is everything all right?"

Puja was the first to answer, "Daddy, I have a boyfriend. I want you to meet him. His name is Juan, and he is attending FIU also. He is so nice. He was waiting in the living room to meet you."

My daughters were quietly waiting for my response. My mind reflected on Puja.

She was obtaining good grades in her classes. She was an obedient and a well-behaved child. Should I object to this new turn in her life?

"Then let us not keep him waiting," I said, jumping out of my bed. Waiting in the living room was my daughter's boyfriend.

He approached me with a smile and said, "Hello, I am Juan. It is a pleasure to meet you, sir." After that first encounter, Puja and Juan became inseparable. Juan became like a member of my family.

He joined us in the temple regularly. Puja's studies and dance sessions did not suffer with the addition of a boyfriend in her life. She became more confident and happier in her life. They spent a lot of time studying together.

Hema said jokingly, "Daddy, you must get a girlfriend. You spend all your time taking care of us. Can, we look for a girlfriend for you?"

I laughed loudly as though I had not laughed for a long time. After a moment of hesitation, I said, "I need to find myself first. Pundit Raj is helping me find myself. When that time comes, it will happen by God's grace," I answered, trying to control my laughter.

Hema was serious—her facial expression showed it—when she said, "Daddy, it is three years since your divorce. It is time to move on with your life. You are mother and father to us, but you should my a girlfriend."

My daughter was lecturing me about relationships; my laughter continued. "Nothing happens before its appointed time. Do not worry about your father. I am happy with my life. One day, a person will come into my life at the right time."

Hema was not happy with my answer.

She hugged me and said, "We worry about you, Daddy. Sometimes, you sit alone and read for hours. You have to go and enjoy the night life."

My simple reply was, "My dear Hema, I am happy with my life. One day, it will happen."

That was the last discussion about my dating. I absorbed myself in my work at the pharmacy, trying to pay the ever-increasing bill payments. My spare time was spent with Puja's dance troupe. Rita and Mena joined us on every road trip.

They became part of my extended family.

We traveled with them as our daughters performed at concerts throughout Florida. It was a joy to see my children adapting to their changing lifestyles and enjoying it.

Most of the shows were for charity programs. In my heart, I was satisfied that Puja was contributing to helping the needy people in her adopted country. Charles Darwin said, "It is not the strongest of the species that survives or the most intelligent that survives. It is the one that is adaptable to change."

My family had adapted well to a foreign land. They had acclimatized themselves with the food, culture, and education. Adaptation is the key to survival.

CHAPTER FOURTEEN

Love Blooms

It was Friday. My pharmacy shift of fourteen exhausting hours was finally coming to a close. My mind was focused on spending the weekend with my three angels. It was about ten in the night. It was closing time for the pharmacy. I was working alone. Suddenly, the doctor's telephone line in the pharmacy rang.

I jumped quickly to answer, "Hurts Rx Pharmacy. This is Pharmacist Moonan speaking. How may I help you?"

My pharmacy supervisor was on the line. "Moonan, whatever you have to do on Saturday and Sunday has to be postponed. You have to work in another store for me. No one is available, so I nominated you to fill the position. Please treat all customers professionally. I do not want to hear any complaints from anyone."

My boss was well known for assigning me to work in other pharmacies without advance notice. My refusal of his sudden demand was out of the question. It meant insubordination, which would lead to my immediate dismissal. He knew that I was not a citizen of this country.

I had a government-issued work permit. This permit was sponsored by the company that employed me. Refusal to work or perform to a high standard will mean immediate dismissal. Most of the times, you are subjected to the whims and fancies of your employer. I wondered whether there was respect for the pharmacist or the pharmacy profession. Therefore, my family will have to return to Trinidad.

"Okay, sir. No problem, sir" was my humble answer. I had planned to spend the weekend with my children. According to my supervisor, "Your work comes first. That is what pays your bills. Everything else in life can be postponed."

At home, my daughters took the bad news half-heartedly. They were accustomed that my employer called and interfered with our prearranged plans.

Saturday morning, I was punctual at my allocated pharmacy. Armed with a book on gardening and my *pelau* for lunch, I prepared myself for another exhausting day. There was no one in the pharmacy to assist me. Working in a different pharmacy was not a problem.

However, every pharmacy was organized differently according to the whims and fancies of the pharmacist/

manager. Therefore, searching for medications is a task by itself.

For the first hour, I was running to attend the customers from the drop-off area to the pick-up area and drive-through area.

An elderly customer politely asked, "Son, how do you manage attending to all these people at the same time? Should a pharmacy have only one person attending to so many patients? That is not safe practice. I know this chain pharmacy makes millions in profits every year, yet the services leave much to be desired.

There are always long lines at their pharmacies, and nothing is done to improve the quality of services. I have been coming to this pharmacy for ten years. Every year, the service gets from bad to worse. This is the closest pharmacy to my home."

The smile from my face was indication enough that she was right on target in her assessment. However, I would have jeopardized my employment if I had given her an honest answer. The honking of a car horn in the drive-through area interrupted our conversation.

Without a second to spare, I rushed to the impatient customer. At the same time, to my relief, a pharmacy technician walked into the pharmacy. Finally, I was getting some much-needed relief.

She introduced herself, saying, "Hello, my name is Clara. I am sorry, but I am not scheduled to work today. The regular technician is sick."

"Ah, I am just glad that you are here. My name is Moonan. I am pleased to meet you. Today, the pharmacy is crazy."

With those words, we hardly spoke for about three hours. We had a smooth coordination of customer service. Her experience and her friendliness were reflected in the high quality of service that she provided to the patients. My priority now was to dispense the patients' medications quickly. Clara was focusing on helping patients to pick up their medications. After about four hours, we were finally able to relax for a few minutes.

I looked at her, and my body was filled with strange emotions. I looked at her left hand. She was wearing a wedding ring. She knew that I was staring at her from head to toe.

After this time, focusing on my work was proving to be a difficult task. I opened my book on gardening to stare at the beautiful flowers. This was to distract my mind from Clara.

As she passed by me, she glanced at the exotic orchids in my book. She then commented, "Wow, that is really pretty! Would you believe that I grow beautiful flowers like these in my home?"

"Are you serious? I love flowers. The beauty of nature relaxes your mind. In the morning, I love to look at the flowers before leaving to work" was my zestful response.

She continued, "I grow only exotic orchids."

She made me so curious about her life. I wondered whether she was married; after all, she had a wedding ring in her hand.

From that evening, we spoke to each other regularly. After work, we departed on our separate ways. That night, Clara was on my mind.

Puja asked, "Daddy, are you okay? You seem to be in a different world. Your mind seems to be preoccupied."

"I am okay," I answered. "Just a little tired."

Puja did not pursue the subject. How could I explain to my daughter my strange feelings?

After all, we had only met for the first time that day. She would think her father is going crazy. In the morning, I returned to the same pharmacy to continue working.

My hopes were high that Clara would be working in the pharmacy that day. At opening time, she walked into the pharmacy with a radiant smile.

"Ah, you are here today. I am glad you came back to work," She said. Then she added, "I never met a guy who liked flowers. I told my daughters that you liked flowers. They laughed and looked at me strangely."

Throughout the day, we spoke freely. The strange feelings inside me had returned on seeing her beautiful, relaxed smile. Luckily for me, the pharmacy was not busy.

We had some free time to talk about our lives. Clara spoke at length about her two daughters. However, she did not mention any husband or man in her life. This was the first time in years that my heart was open to someone. The important question still lingered: Was she married?

The only way was to be blunt. There was nothing to lose from such a question. "Clara," I asked with hesitation, "are you married?"

She laughed loudly and said, "No, I was divorced years ago. I wear the ring to prevent people from hitting on me. Why do you ask?"

"Then, can I come and take a look at your exotic orchids?" She hesitated and then said, "Okay, after work today is fine."

After closing the pharmacy, we drove in our separate cars to her home. My impression of this lady was further exalted when I viewed some of the rarest orchids. Her house was surrounded by the most colorful orchids.

On my cell phone, I took the most beautiful photos. We shared telephone numbers and promised to call each other. She called about four days later. "Hey, Moonan, how are you? Listen, I am going Orlando to my sister's home. I will call you again. I will return on Sunday night. Bye."

I told her, "Enjoy your trip. Be careful on the road."

With that parting farewell, she would call me numerous times on her journey to Orlando. I asked myself, *Why did she call me about three times? Is she developing emotional feelings for me?* My feelings for her were certainly getting stronger every moment.

About two in the morning, my cell phone rang in the living room. Puja answered my telephone with a puzzled look. Her face lit up. "Daddy, there is a girl on the phone for you at this time."

It was Clara on the telephone. "Hey, who is that woman on the phone? Are you married, and you did not tell me?"

"No, no," I said, laughing, "like you; I was divorced a long time ago. My three daughters live with me. I have no girlfriend at the present time. When you return to Miami, please come and visit us."

Then Clara gave me some hope; she said, "That is good to hear. Take care of yourself. Anyway, I have reached safely by my sister's. Goodnight."

Sunday night, before Clara returned from Orlando, I placed a vase of roses at her front door. My daughters had noticed that my face had a special glow. After having been divorced for three years, my heart was finally pulsating to start a new personal relationship.

On her return from Orlando, Clara saw the roses at her front door.

She called, "You know, this is so thoughtful of you. No guy has given me roses for the longest time. I really appreciate these roses. You make me feel very special."

Those words energized my heart. My body was invigorated.

I added, "Can I invite you sometime to Bahama Breeze for dinner?"

"Yes, but not this week. I am working all week. The following Sunday after work, we can have dinner. You can call me," she added.

We met by pure coincidence. Both of us were not scheduled to work that weekend. Had fate brought us together?

Nicholas Sparks is quoted as saying, "There is winds of destiny that blow when we least expect them. Sometimes, they gust with the fury of a hurricane, sometimes they barely fan one's cheek. But the winds cannot be denied, bringing, as they often do, a future that is impossible to ignore."

The week flew by quickly. The appointed time for my long-awaited date was here. My heart was fluttering like a teenager on his first date on reaching her front door.

Pundit Raj had taught me the art of relaxing by using deep breathing exercises. I took a deep relaxed breath and knocked on the door. Emerging from behind the door was the most beautiful woman. She wore a beautiful black dress with matching ornaments. She had a heart-warming smile. I stuttered for words. "Goodnight. How are you? My goodness, you look utterly beautiful! This single red rose is for you."

"Thank you," she said, smiling.

During our drive to Bahama Breeze, I said, "Tell me about yourself. What country you came from?"

"My life is all work. I have two children. My sister lives in Orlando. I am from the Dominican Republic. All my family lives there. The country is extremely beautiful. The beaches are out of this world," she answered.

I told her about myself without sounding boring.

You can call this my first date in Florida. We enjoyed the food at the restaurant.

After the meal, we sat and spoke until it was closing time. I held her hand as we departed from the restaurant. We mutually agreed to see each other again.

After our fourth date and one month later, I told her jokingly, "You will fall in love with me. I am going to steal your heart. You are going to love me".

She laughed heartily without answering and continue laughing for a few minutes. She thought that statement was really funny.

Now it was time to introduce our family. After one month, my children were curious about my mystery date. One day, we stopped at her workplace, and I introduced my children to Clara. She was busy in the pharmacy. We waited patiently for her.

She rushed out to meet us for a few minutes.

"Hello, I am surprised to meet you here. I just have a minute to talk to you," she said, looking at a line of customers waiting for her attention.

"These are my daughters—Hema, Puja, and Mala. We were just in the neighborhood, and I just passed to introduce my children. Anyway, I brought a single rose for you."

"Thank you. That is so sweet of you. However, I have to return to the pharmacy and help the customers. Goodbye and thank you," she said, planting a gentle kiss on my cheek. My brown face illuminated with passion for her.

I was aware that this was the wrong time for personal conversations. She said salutations to my family, and we departed from the pharmacy.

In my vehicle, Puja said jokingly with piercing eyes, "Daddy, you know, since your divorce, this is the first time that you have introduced us to a female friend. What is going on here? Do I smell love in the air?"

I laughed and said, "Time will tell, my dear. Time will certainly tell. What you smell is food. I think that you are hungry."

That night, my mind was busy analyzing my newfound friendship. Both of us were single parents. We had parental custody of our children. Our passions were similar: gardening, cooking, and fishing. Our abstinence from alcohol and cigarettes were the same.

Yet we belonged to two different cultures. My pundit (or teacher) from Trinidad had told me, "This body is a shell. The real person lies deep inside their physical body. Take time to discover the true person.

Cultures can merge to see a larger picture of life. Cooperation and understanding is the key to a successful relationship.

Learn from her culture, for it makes you a better person. Physical attributes are maya (or illusion)." One day, Clara called and said, "Moonan, I wanted to invite your family to my home on Sunday for dinner."

I realized then that Clara had similar feelings for me even though she never admitted it. That Sunday, I met her two daughters. Both of them were nice and friendly.

My three daughters were chatting comfortably with her two daughters. Her eldest daughter was accompanied by her boyfriend. This was a good sign for me.

Then Clara invited us to Orlando to meet her sister Marianna and family. The members of her family were very accommodating and down to earth. We were given a very friendly welcome. Marianna cooked my favorite Hispanic dish, *paella*.

I prepared for them some Indian dishes like roti and *saheena*. They love the flavor of the food. Clara's family was very family oriented. Like my family, they were very close-knit. It was a pleasure meeting her family in Orlando. We returned to Miami.

The time to renew work permit or visas was here again. In order to renew our application, we had to travel to the United States Embassy in Trinidad. This would mean my absence from Clara for two weeks. She understood our situation.

Clara gave my family a ride to Miami International Airport. It was heart-breaking saying good-bye to Clara. As we departed, tears flowed from her eyes.

She sincerely said, "I love you. I will miss you every day. You are part of my life now. Take care of yourself. Call me every day. Give my love to your family."

My smile told my story. "You are part of my life now. I love you. Take care of yourself." We embraced and kissed as if it was our last farewell. Tears came into our eyes.

Puja's boyfriend, Juan, was at the airport, saying his farewell to our family. His eyes were full of tears. I wondered whether my Puja was in love. Then was his love for Puja very sincere? As a single parent, you learn to protect your children more closely.

They are now inseparable. It was a sad farewell. Puja was silent throughout the flight to Trinidad. It was unlike Puja to be so quiet.

I asked myself the same question: Is my Puja in love? We all sat together on the flight; only Puja was quiet. It was expensive to travel very often to Trinidad with my family.

At the Piarco International Airport in Trinidad, we were greeted with the same royalty welcome like our last visit. After greeting everyone in Trinidad, Clara was on my mind. From my brother's cell phone, I called to inform her that our flight had landed in Trinidad. There was no answer.

I knew Puja was waiting to call Juan. She had a serious and worried countenance.

Early Monday morning, my family reached the United States Embassy. We were informed that our visas would take an extra week to process instead of the previous time. In addition, my work permit would only be extended for one year instead of the regular two years.

The look of frustration and disappointment was apparent in Puja's face. She was missing Juan. In addition, she had to miss a few classes at FIU. I telephoned my supervisor at Hurts Rx Pharmacy, and he was very upset about my situation.

With these latest developments, I requested Jewan, my son, to carry us to Maracas Beach. No one spoke on our drive through the fabulous landscape to Maracas Beach. Everyone was sad and depressed.

Two years ago, my children stopped along the same route to take numerous pictures of the scenic landscapes. Hema and Puja were then boasting of their photography skills. We stopped to buy the world's famous bake and shark on Maracas Beach. Not a word was spoken by anyone.

This silence was killing me. Can we do anything about the situation?

If we are upset, is it going to help our problem?

We have to accept this unforeseen dilemma and work around it.

I called my boss and explained the latest developments. He was not happy, but what could I have done?

Puja e-mailed FIU and informed them. "If you can, do some make-up classes. Hema, you have to do the same. Let us make the best of the unforeseen circumstances and enjoy ourselves."

With those words, everyone became more talkative. We enjoyed the soothing clear waters of Maracas Beach just like two years ago. Coming to Maracas Beach was not our agenda. However, having received bad news, it was necessary to soothe the minds of my children.

We headed back to my parents' home in Caroni Village.

They were anxiously awaiting the outcome of our visa applications. Their approach to our problem was more positive than our opinion. My father added, "We are getting old, my son.

At least, you can spend more time with the old folks here. Everything happens for the best. This is a good time for you to enjoy yourself. Remember, before you leave, we have to perform a prayer for your family."

That night, I finally found the time to speak to both my parents on my relationship with Clara. There was a glow in my face when I said, "After having been divorced for three years, I finally found someone that I truly love. We have a good understanding."

My father asked, "Do you really love her? Do you have a photo of her?"

"Yes, Dad. Here is her photo. She was born in the Dominican Republic. She lives in Miami."

I handed him her photo. My parents examined the photograph closely.

My mother said, "Remember, with love comes dignity and respect for each other's cultures. My family has traveled from India to Trinidad. My children are now living in Canada, United States, Grenada, and Dominican Republic.

Everyone has a different journey in life. The hearts are the same.

Life is difficult, but with a companion by your side, it is a blessing. We are linked to the Baijoo name. Beta (or son), I am very happy that you have found a true companion. Love is not color or race. Love is from the heart. When you are a husband, you have to live up to that sacred title.

Take your duty and commitment as a husband seriously.

One day, you have to give an account for your loyalty as a husband to God.

Therefore, the commitment to marriage should not be taken lightly."

We spent a long time talking about love and relationships.

"Then you have our blessings. No one can come to the wedding because we do not one have visas for traveling. You have my family blessings.

Wherever you go, you will find racial or biased people. Do not stoop to their level. Rise above discrimination, then you are not a living dead in society," my father added.

My son Jewan was waiting patiently for me.

Jewan and I would spend all night talking at the University of the West Indies. He started, "Your migration to the United States has made my life a little more complicated. However, I have adjusted to your absence here. This is my final year of studies at our university. There so many things that I want to achieve. However, within financial constrains, my further education is also important."

That day, I allowed my son to talk about his dreams and aspirations. My idea was to listen to all his plans and dreams. We were separated for a long time, but I felt connected to him.

"What about a girlfriend?" was my question.

He laughed heartily at eluding this delicate topic and then said, "Yes and no, but I do not know. At this stage, I am not sure. Time will tell."

From the university, we headed to a roadside barbeque. The food was delicious. The sun was rising as we headed to my parents' home.

My brothers were waiting for my arrival. They were prepared to go fishing.

My eldest brother shouted, "Hey, man, we are waiting for you to go fishing in the Biche forest! Just jump in. We have extra clothes for you. We will buy some breakfast on the way for you."

Without hesitation, I jumped into their waiting vehicle.

Biche forest is mainly an agricultural area. Some of the best coffee and cocoa are grown here. It is one of the most friendly areas in Trinidad.

The area is well known for the largest snakes like the Everglades in Florida.

Our prized fishes, the cascadura, live abundantly in the Biche area. Our relationships with my brothers were rekindled.

We spoke about the good old days about working in the sugarcane fields and planting rice. However, our conversation was foremost about fishing.

As a team, we have fished in these forest many times. That day, we were fortunate that we caught about 800 large cascaduras. As brothers, we have a passion of boasting about the size of our catch. Of course, this is a good feast for our Christmas festivities.

Christmas season is here again. The holiday season brings all families, friends, and neighbors closer together.

Everyone was invited to all the neighbors' homes. Interestingly, in Trinidad, every home celebrates Christmas regardless of religion. With all the partying, my thoughts strayed with my new love in Miami.

Clara was working, so it was difficult to reach her on the telephone. Finally, she answered her telephone, "Hello, my dear, I miss you. I love you. We have to return to Miami one week later. I called my boss, but he was very upset. My family desperately wants to see you."

Clara was excited to hear my voice. "I realized the holidays are not the same without you. I love you. Everything here is all right. I am looking forward to your return."

We spoke until the telephone card was completely utilized.

Our visas came in the mail. The next day, we returned to Miami to face all our outstanding issues. Clara and Juan were anxiously awaiting our arrival at the Miami Airport terminal. On seeing Clara and Juan, I realized that they were not just friends but our new family in Florida. This was an emotional reunion. There were tears of joys.

After our reunion, my first call was to my supervisor at Hurts Rx Pharmacy.

He was abrupt on the telephone. "The days that you were absent, you will definitely not be paid. Take two more days off again. Then return to work."

I answered, "Thank you, sir. Thank you very much."

As Clara reached my house, she said, "My dear, I cannot stay and chat. I have work in the pharmacy early in the morning."

We kissed and then departed. Juan stayed to spend time with Puja.

I tried calling my son, but the telephone was dead. There was no water coming in our taps at my home.

I fell on my bed and slept peacefully until the morning. My pharmacy supervisor had given me two extra days leave. In a way, it gave me time to call the authorities to help restore my water and telephone services.

America is now my home; there is no turning back. Clara and I had been dating for about three years. In the silence of my bedroom, my thoughts were running through all the wonderful times we shared. The question was, did I want to spend the rest of my life with Clara?

Armed with a bouquet of flowers, I headed for Clara's house.

I knocked on her door, and she came out smiling.

"Will you marry me?" was the question as I placed the bouquet of flowers in her hands.

Clara was at a loss for words. Her face glowed with happiness. The following week, we were married in civil ceremony in Downtown Miami.

Two weeks later, on Valentine's Day, we had a big reception at our home.

It was a lavish ceremony. We invited a lot of friends and family. The buffet was a wide variety from American, Arabic, Indian, Chinese, and Hispanic foods.

Speeches were given with translation in English, Spanish, Arabic, and Hindi.

From the Bible, 1 Corinthians 13:7—

"Love never gives up, never loses faith, is always hopeful, and endures through every circumstance."

Clara's mother and family came from Dominican Republic. In the presence of my new wife, I asked Clara's mother to bless our marriage. She said a prayer for our blessing. Our blissful honeymoon was spent at the Marriott Hotel.

During our new life, we traveled to Trinidad to see my family. This was our first vacation as husband and wife.

Clara was unusually quiet on our flight to Trinidad.

I poked her gently and said, "My dear, you are now married, but you look very worried. Can you share your problem with me?"

After a minute, Clara held my hand tightly and responded sadly, "I am Hispanic. I know little of your culture. What will your family think about me?"

I laughed loudly, and the nearby passengers glared at me. "Do me a favor. Just be yourself. You love me. They will love you for that alone."

We spent four tranquil days in Trinidad. Clara loved every minute with my family.

As we departed from Trinidad, my eldest brother hugged her and wept bitterly. His advice to my wife was, "Make Moonan happy, and we will be happy."

We also traveled to Las Vegas and Dominican Republic. It was a joyful time spent in Dominican Republic.

Our time together was heavenly. We enjoyed each other's company. Love was in the air.

One year later, Juan and Puja were married in a civil ceremony. Both had finished their studies at their university. Puja was now a registered nurse.

Love was contagious. Soon, my step daughter was married to her Haitian boyfriend.

1 Corinthians 13:4-8—

Love is patient and kind.

Love does not envy or boast.

It is not arrogant or rude.

Love does not insist on its own way.

Love bears all things, believes all things, and endures all things.

Love never ends.

04.07.2009

Beautiful flowers growing in my yard.

Beautiful flowers growing in my yard.

CHAPTER FIFTEEN

Capturing the American Dream

It was more than eleven years since working at Hurts Rx Pharmacy. My new female supervisor was not happy with my performance. None of my pharmacy staff had been reprimanded except me for alleged poor performance. On the contrary, Hurts Rx Pharmacy awarded me with the biggest bonus for excellent store performance. They also rewarded me with company shares and stocks for meeting all their highest expectations. At the company level I am rewarded.

At the store level, nothing seemed to satisfy my new pharmacy supervisor. Strangely, none of my superiors in the past eleven years had ever complained about my personal performance. On the contrary, they loved my level of good service Now, even as a professional, I am traumatized by her presence in my pharmacy.

One day, at home, Clara observed that I was sitting on the veranda and staring at the clouds without saying a word.

She knows like my children that we are talkative by nature. She passed her finger through my hair and enquired, "Hey baby, you are usually quiet. Are you sick today?"

I pondered for a minute, then took a deep breath and answered, "My boss will fire me sooner or later. She is never upset with anyone of my staff except me. She smiles and talks with them very pleasantly, then chastises me for frivolous things. On a few occasions, she has threatened to fire me. I can feel it in my bones. Her charges are broad-based and untrue. My job definitely is in jeopardy."

Clara's facial expression changed to one of sadness.

"Are you joking, or is it your arthritis that is acting up? Do not worry. You receive numerous compliments from your customers. All these compliments are seen by your corporate office. All your pharmacy metrics are excellent. These are sent by your head office. What is the problem? In this district, eighty percent of the stores are not performing as good as your pharmacy."

After a minute of silence, my answer was very profound.

"Sometimes, people are just haters. I have sacrificed a lot for this company. Every day I reach my pharmacy one hour before opening hours. Then I will stay after hours to complete unfinished assignments without any monetary compensations. My family has suffered tremendously because of my devotion and commitment to my profession.

The American Dream

I am a team player in the best interest of Hurts Rx Pharmacy. My concerns about this trauma, for being fired, was addressed to our Human Resources Department. Nothing was brought to her attention.

"My personal services to every customer are beyond question. It will be a sad day for the profession to fire an outstanding and exemplary worker."

My premonition was true. Two weeks later, my blonde supervisor fired me without any compensation. Sadly, not one of my devious staff spoke on my behalf. For the last five years, they were my adopted family. My humble answer to my boss was, "This termination is not based on my nonperformance. For the last year, my pharmacy achieved high scores at every level. Your decision is not professional but more personal. God will have his way. God bless you."

Mahatma Gandhi put it simply,

"There is no God higher than truth".

Previously, for nonperformance, Hurts Rx Pharmacy would demote you to a floater pharmacist. That option was not given to me. No compensation was offered for years of sacrifice and devoted service to this wonderful company.

There is life after Hurts Rx Pharmacy. These are the "living dead" people that my father told me so many times.

Walter Anderson said, "Bad things do happen; how I respond to them defines my character and the quality of my life. I can choose to sit in perpetual sadness, immobilized by the gravity of my loss, or I can choose to rise from the pain and treasure the most precious gift I have—life itself."

After capturing the American dream, I felt for a moment it flew away from my grasp.

I felt betrayed that none of my staff stood to my defense, especially my staff pharmacists.

Life always offers you alternatives and solutions. New opportunities are always waiting like the silver lining in the clouds. We just have to seize the right moment.

This was a good time to take a much-needed vacation. Time resolves all problems; just add a little patience.

My friends encouraged me to apply for unemployment benefits.

After working in United States for more than twelve years, unemployment benefits was not my option. My ego would not accept that option.

After the news of my termination, my mind was angry as I drove away from Hurts Rx Pharmacy. I felt violated without a just cause. One person was tarnishing the image of this great and vibrant company.

Dr. Maria, my Hispanic mother, had previously called on my cell phone. She had sensed that everything was not right with her adopted son. As I drove away from the pharmacy, Dr. Maria called again. The traumatic news about my demise was not taken easily by my adopted mother. My mentor and friend was very extremely upset. "You are an American. You must stand up for your rights. Do not let anyone walk over you. Keep your head up high. You did nothing that required your dismissal. You are the best at what you do. You have a passion for serving people. Anyway, when one door closes, more opens. I am watching your back. My advice to you is to take a week's vacation. I will help you get a work. Do not worry."

My father had said, "We must be humble. As a people, we are very humble, but do not mistake humility for weakness. People, by nature, are very cruel and abusive. You may not get a promotion because of your race or beliefs. When your rights are trampled, then stand up for your rights."

In the Bible, Matthew 18:4 says, "Therefore, anyone who humbles himself as this little child is the greatest in the kingdom of heaven."

Be humble but strong was the message from my father and Dr. Maria.

My mentor also suggested that I needed a week's vacation from the pharmacy environment.

Therefore, the next day, I was fishing alone from the scenic Key Biscannye Bridge in Miami.

As I inhaled the fresh sea breeze, my mind flew back to my past experiences, even to the perilous journey my forefathers undertook from Bihar, India, to Trinidad. Staring at the vast expanse of ocean, it was difficult to comprehend the dangers of such a journey. Without proper accommodations on a boat, they were at the mercy of the elements of nature and their colonial masters.

They were merely a commodity or merchandise to be traded to the highest bidder. My forefathers were taking a dangerous trip to improve the quality of their lives.

Even while working in the sugarcane fields, they encouraged their children to improve their lives. None of my family remains working in the sugarcane fields. Migration was an alternative to improve the quality of their lives. My brother and his family now live happily in Canada. One of my sisters lives in the beautiful island of Grenada. Daily in the media, we hear about people fleeing their countries in primitive modes of transport, trying desperately to reach the shores of the United States.

The American Dream

Sometimes, they flee because of political persecutions in desperate search of a better way of life.

Others just try to capture the American dream at all cost. The upsurge in crime was the major criteria for fleeing from the beloved Trinidad. My family journey to this country was full of intrigue and drama. When my family reached the beautiful shores of Florida, my hopes of employment were shattered by broken false promises. My new friend, Moe, was instrumental in securing a job in a small family oriented pharmacy. I walked six miles daily to my work.

There were no buses traveling on my route. Very often, my clothes were drenched from the friendly Florida showers. After failing my State Board Examination, my second chance led to success. Financially, my life was now more secured than the previous years. When you think that your life is on the upswing, divorce sneaks upon you like a thief in the night. All my finances were exhausted with the onslaught of my divorce requirements. My solution for survival was to work extraneous hours to meet my financial commitments, or go to jail. After years of sacrifice and savings, my daughters and I eventually bought a small home. In today's market, it is overvalued and overpriced. One year after purchasing my home, Hurricanes Wilma and Katrina followed, with devastating effect. Slowly, the rebuilding process began until our little castle was restored to suitable living standards. Three years after my divorce, love came knocking at my heart's door. We eventually got married and are happy together after years.

Through the goodness and kindness of the American Government, we are now citizens in this great land. United States is a melting pot of many cultures. At the end of the road, we are all American with a commitment to serving this sacred land. My family had truly evolved from, adapted to, and captured the American dream.

My two eldest daughters had graduated from colleges. In Trinidad, Jewan, my son, graduated from the university with first-class honors. Sadly, I was unable to attend his graduation. Puja is now married to Juan. They renewed their vows in a fairy-tale wedding in Palmetto Bay. It was extremely fortunate that Jewan came for this special occasion. His wedding toast was emotional and inspirational. My advice to this young couple was, "You have merged two of the greatest cultures in the world. Embrace them and pass that knowledge to your children."

They bought their dream house in a quiet neighborhood.

What is the elusive American dream?

James Adams wrote, "Life should be better and richer and fuller for everyone, with opportunity for each according to ability or achievement."

My drive to prosper in Florida solidifies the foundation for building my American dream.

Our Declaration of Independence states, "All men are created equal, that they are endowed by their Creator with certain unalienable rights, that among these are life, liberty, and the pursuit of happiness."

To the millions of American immigrants, this dream is not elusive.

It takes time, patience, courage, and sacrifice to conquer and reach your goals. My journey does not end here. It is a new and solid beginning. It is a journey into the life of every immigrant who endure hardships daily to keep their families together. A united family is a united America.

My wife and I

My Son and I

My Grandson and Family

Fourth of July Celebration

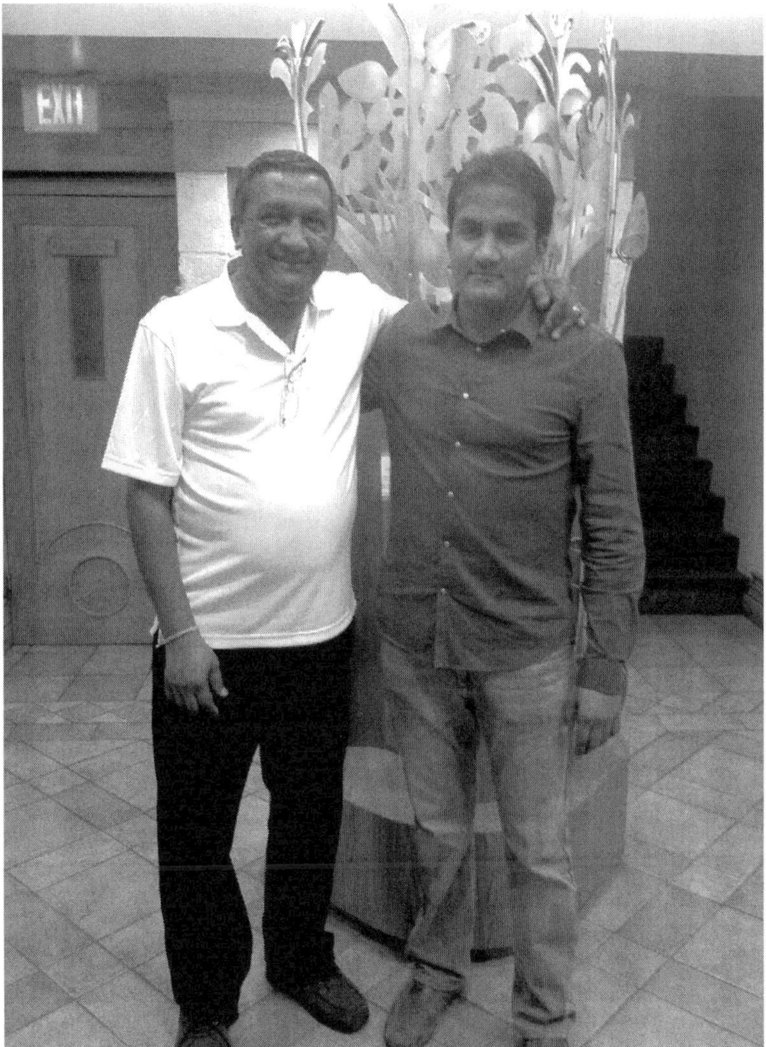

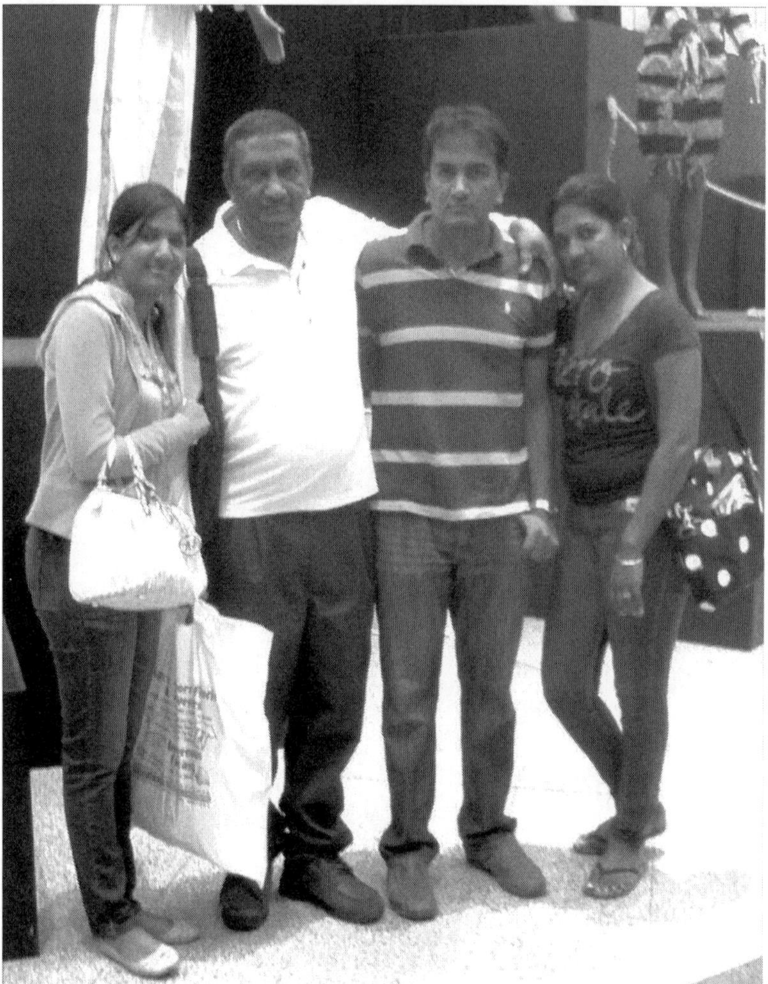

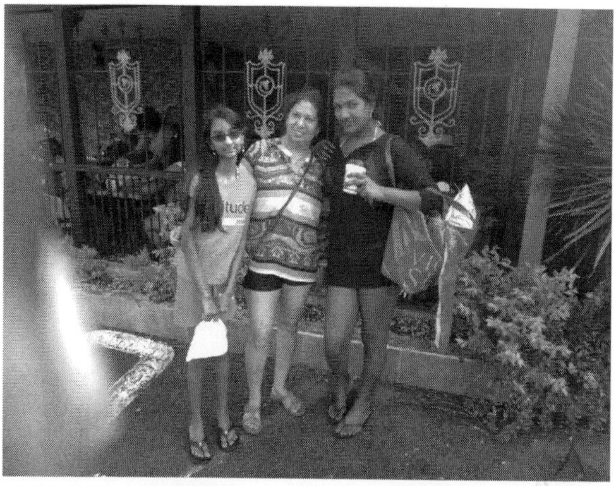

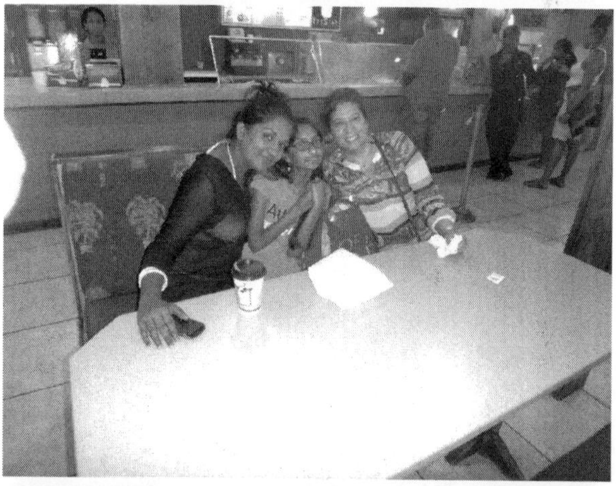

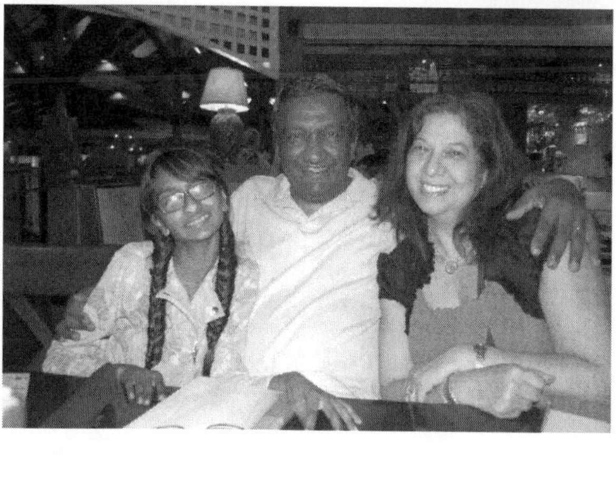

GLOSSARY

- *Adios* is a Spanish phrase, meaning good-bye or farewell.
- *Adios amigo* means "Good-bye, my friend."
- *Bhai* means brother in Hindi. Bhai-ji means respected brother.
- Bollywood is the term used to describe the film industry in India. They produce more films than Hollywood.
- *Buenos dias* is a Spanish phrase, meaning good day or good morning. *Buenos noches* means good night.
- Calypso originated in Trinidad and Tobago. It is a distinct Afro-Caribbean music. It is popular at Carnival time where big competitions are common. Trinidad and Tobago is known as the land of steel band and calypso.
- Cascadura is a freshwater catfish. This fish is a delicacy in the Caribbean islands, especially Trinidad. The meat is the sweetest among fishes.
- Chutney is a music art form created by Indo-Caribbean people whose ancestors came from Bihar and Uttar Pradesh. The music has a spicy rhythm or a dance vibration. The artists use a combination of Indian instruments like harmonium, dhantal, and dholak with electric guitars and synthesizers. *Chutney* is also used to describe a spicy condiment.

- *Como esta usted?* This is a very popular Spanish phrase. Translated in English, it means "How are you?"
- *Hola* is a Spanish term that means hello. *Hola mi amor* means "Hello, my love."
- Islamic term: Assalaamu alaikum. This is a common greeting among Muslims. It means, "May peace be upon you." The correct response is "Wa alaikum assalaam," which means "And upon you be peace also."
- *Muy bien, gracias* is a Spanish phrase, meaning, "Very well, thank you."
- *Namaste* or *Namaskar* is an East Indian custom of respectful greeting. The hands are clasped together in a prayerful fashion in front of the chest area, and there is a slight bow of the head. It basically means "I bow to the divine (God) in you."
- *Nana* and *nani* are Hindi terms used to describe grandfather and grandmother.
- *Neemakaram* is a Hindi word that basically means "ungrateful to the lowest degree." It is a very degrading term.
- *Paella* is a mouth-watering Spanish dish. It is a combination of rice, meat, seafoods, vegetables, and beans. Two key ingredients are saffron and olive oil. There is a lot of variation to this recipe.
- *Pelau* is a savory, spicy, one-pot Trinidad dish. It is a combination of protein, carbs, and vegetables cooked all

in one pot. This is a favorite dish when cooking food by the riverside, beach, or any big party.
- *Puja*, simply translated, means prayer. It covers a variety of prayers.
- *Roti* is derived from a Sanskrit word, meaning bread. Like bread, there are a lot of different types of roti.
- *Saheena* is an East Indian delicacy. It is served as a snack for all occasions. It is a vegetarian dish made mainly from spinach. It is a very healthy snack.
- Satan was an angel who rebelled against God in the Bible. He is portrayed as evil. His name is used to describe a wicked person.

Made in the USA
San Bernardino, CA
13 June 2014